# Oriental Rugs
## The Secrets Revealed

### Mark Blackburn

## DEDICATION

This book is dedicated to all the sheep of the world;
without them the following pages would not have
been possible.

**Other Schiffer Books by Mark Blackburn:**
*Hawaiiana: The Best of Hawaiian Design*
*Hula Girls & Surfer Boys*
*Hula Heaven: The Queen's Album*
*Tattoos From Paradise*

**Special Thanks to:**
Tom Major
Matthew Auker

### A Word About The Rugs Pictured In This Book

We have made an attempt to show rugs here that are currently available in the marketplace, not fantasy rugs or categories that are currently on their way out of fashion and production, such as Indo Persian rugs and sculptured Chinese rugs, just to give you two examples. Due to rising costs in all areas where carpets are produced and a lack of interest in the market, several types of rugs that were popular just a few years ago are in limited production or are no longer being made at all. Therefore, we show just a few examples of those rugs in the following pages.

Library of Congress Cataloging-in-Publication Data

Blackburn, Mark.
  Oriental rugs : the secrets revealed / Mark Blackburn.
    p. cm.
  ISBN 978-0-7643-2641-7 (hardcover)
  1. Rugs, Oriental. I. Title.

NK2808.B63 2007
746.7'5--dc22
                              2006103306

Designed by John P. Cheek
Cover design by Bruce Waters
Type set in Allembert/Souvenir Lt BT

ISBN: 978-0-7643-2641-7
Printed in China

Published by Schiffer Publishing Ltd.
4880 Lower Valley Road
Atglen, PA 19310
Phone: (610) 593-1777; Fax: (610) 593-2002
E-mail: Info@schifferbooks.com

For the largest selection of fine reference books on this and related subjects, please visit our web site at
**www.schifferbooks.com**
We are always looking for people to write books on new and related subjects.
If you have an idea for a book please contact us at the above address.

This book may be purchased from the publisher.
Include $3.95 for shipping.
Please try your bookstore first.
You may write for a free catalog.

In Europe, Schiffer books are distributed by
Bushwood Books
6 Marksbury Ave.
Kew Gardens
Surrey TW9 4JF England
Phone: 44 (0) 20 8392-8585;
Fax: 44 (0) 20 8392-9876
E-mail: info@bushwoodbooks.co.uk
Website: www.bushwoodbooks.co.uk
Free postage in the U.K., Europe; air mail at cost.

# Contents

# Preface

**Hooked rugs** are made by pushing and looping yarn through a canvas. Popular in country settings, they have their origins in folk America.

---

**Braided** rugs are a uniquely American product made by braiding yarns or used fabric around a core and shaping it into a oval shape.

People always ask me, "How did you get started in the rug business?" I tell them, by trying to be an educated consumer. It all started like this… Over 30 years ago, my wife and I were in the market for an Oriental rug, which should have been fairly simple enough. We figured out our size requirements and general color palette, and off we went "rug shopping."

We were living in Santa Fe, New Mexico, at the time, so we had plenty of sources to scour. The first shop we walked into was a very typical, high-pressure affair. Immediately we felt intimidated. Like rapid fire, a litany of questions was drilled right at us. All of which came down to two simple questions: What size are you looking for and how much do you want to spend?

We had only been in the establishment a matter of a few minutes when this sales approach was used…basically trying to force us into looking and buying. We stayed a very short time and saw a rug of Turkish design that we liked, a traditional 6' x 9' Hereke pattern. The price tag indicated that it was $6,000 but was now reduced to $4,000. At the time it was out of our budget, so we politely said thank you and proceeded to exit. Then we were bombarded with, "we can give you a better price for today only as its our first sale of the day and it was bad luck to not give a generous discount to such a fine young couple." End of story.

A couple of hours passed and we went into another store, this time operated by two New Yorkers who were passing themselves off as some type of rug merchant in from the desert. In this situation, at least, the pressure to buy was somewhat less and the rugs were being sold in an outdoor setting. We found a similar Hereke rug from

Turkey, in the same size, and the price was now $2,700. We were blown away by this. In fact, it was virtually the same rug we had seen earlier in the day, but cost $3,300 off the first store's price. (Even with their "special sale" it was $1,300 less.) Needless to say, I was flabbergasted by this experience, as I had never seen such a wide swing in prices. But the story does not end here. The couple from New York immediately put on the pressure, resulting in our leaving their open-air establishment.

The next day we went to Albuquerque on another errand and happened to see a large rug store with "GO-ING OUT OF BUSINESS" signs everywhere. How could we resist? Here was a real opportunity, maybe, to find our carpet at a greatly discounted price. Upon entering the store, we were quite literally besieged by salesmen who battered us with questions. This now made our previous experiences in the other two establishments a walk in the park. After a short time, we told the proprietor and his sales force we were looking for a Hereke from Turkey, in approximately 6' x 9' size. Within a minute or two, several helpers threw onto the showroom floor an almost identical rug to the ones we had seen in Santa Fe, but now the price was $24,000. But, they told us, it was 80% off, resulting in an unbelievable price of $4,800. Talk about shock; we were in total disbelief and immediately exited that establishment, too, only to be followed to our car where we were told that if we took it right now, we could have it for another 25% off, making it $3,600. At this point, we no longer wanted to look for a carpet again, until…

As a broker in precious metals, I had frequent occasions to fly to Switzerland on business. On one such trip there, over a long holiday weekend, I decided to pop over to Istanbul for a couple of days until I had to return to Zurich. So off I went, on a trip that changed my life forever.

I stayed at the Istanbul Hilton and decided to take a stroll down the street to the Grand Bazaar. Once inside, I was in an Arabian nights dream, surrounded by sights and sounds of Eastern commerce. Everywhere I looked there were carpets, merchants, glass and brass vendors, spice shops, etc. After the initial shock of this foreign world, I entered a carpet shop where, in a very short time, I found the Hereke carpet we had seen in New Mexico, but for a price less than $800 in the equivalent currency. After some tea and a hour of negotiating, I purchased the carpet for $600 - the rest of the story is history.

In a nutshell, it was this experience that led me to my profession as a rug dealer. After years of dealing in commodities and working on very close margins, I figured, why not treat carpets the same way, buy them in large quantities and mark them up only a very small percentage?

After a trial run in Santa Fe, where I converted my wife's boutique into a rug store, we decided to relocate to historic Lancaster County, Pennsylvania, which at the time was the seventh largest tourist destination in the country.

I opened a "rug outlet" to offer fine quality, hand-made rugs to the general mid-Atlantic area, from a farm field on U.S. Route 30. The location has greatly changed in over 22 years since we started, but that is how it all began.

Now, after many months spent overseas over many years, after buying and selling tens of thousands of rugs, I can truly tell the inside story of the carpet trade. It is a story that has really not been told in such depth before.

Carpets are a real joy; they are art for the floor that will enhance any home environment, truly a unique art form in every way. Not only do they provide pleasure to all, but warmth and, as Edgar Alan Poe once said, "The soul of the apartment is the rug."

# The Secrets Revealed

Oriental rugs have been made for 2,000 or more years. A discovery in a Scythain burial mound in the last century proved this, with the discovery of the "Pazyrk" carpet, which was a fragment of a pile carpet dating to the fifth century B.C. Other fragments have also surfaced, proving that carpet weaving was widespread throughout the Near and Middle East. It was known in the Byzantine Empire, at the least in the beginning of the first millennium. With the discovery of wall paintings in Khocho, the capital of the Ulgur Turks in Eastern Turkestan, there is the suggestion that the craft was fully developed in Central Asia as well, before the advent of Islam in the year 600 A.D.

Rugs created by Nomads to furnish their tents also served to fulfill a need for artistic expression. Many of these original design elements and concepts have remained embodied in traditional carpets today date back to these original nomadic traditions. Techniques and designs were perfectly suited to the purpose of these early weavers and were perpetuated as folk art as long as their tribal way of life was preserved. However, with time, the designs of carpets had to be adapted and transformed as they are today to the market place and its needs. The first real transformation was for the needs of Oriental potentates to fill their palaces and their great religious establishments. Artists of various callings became involved in designing carpets befitting both the demands of their powerful patrons and the majestic proportions of their commissions. Soon schools flourished dedicated to all the Islamic arts and it can be said with certainty that at this time the carpet joined the main stream of Islamic culture and life.

Islam became widespread after its inception and the faith quickly spread throughout the Near East and Central Asia. In a relatively short time, this powerful religious idea linked the people of many countries from present day Spain to China. Soon, a great flourish of artistic endeavors followed. Many of these highly developed cultural traditions, long established in some of these areas, played an important role in fashioning the distinctive style which emerged and set its seal on all arts and crafts in the Islamic world, especially so in rug weaving. It is from these ancient traditions that the modern-day Oriental rug has evolved.

## Rug Production

To start making a rug, the wool must be removed from the sheep. It is the first step in the long and tedious process of rug weaving. For the sake of beauty and quality, the weaving technique must be carried out as perfectly as possible. There are over a hundred varieties of sheep in the world. Wool taken from various breeds and parts of the animal also determine the quality of the finished product. After the wool has been removed with the use of scissors or similar tools, it is carefully washed, dried, and combed. At this point, the wool is then painstakingly handspun, using a hand-turned spindle to create yarn of a desired ply and strength. Today, in some cases, the wool is spun with the use of automated machines, resulting in a more uniform look and achieving a clearer and tighter design in the finished product. Personally, I enjoy the look of handspun wool, which tends to make the finished rug more irregular in its pile, often resulting in the knots being more visible throughout the face or top of the rug.

The next step is to dye the yarn in the various colors desired. First, the wool is carefully boiled to remove any excess impurities in a mordant bath.

Dyeing wool yarn, Peshawar, Pakistan.

After this procedure, the yarn is placed in another large container and boiled with the desired dye for several hours.

A hot dyeing vat, Peshawar, Pakistan.

**Abrash** is a term that refers to the inconsistent color or hue found in both new and antique rugs. The variations in color are usually the result of dyeing the wool at different times or in batches thus resulting in a beautiful variation in color hues. It is primarily prevalent in carpets made with vegetal dyes. Today the top three machine made rug manufacturers have artificially added this look to their copies to give their rugs a more realistic look, paling in comparison and durability to the genuine article.

**Mordants** are metallic salts used to attach various natural dyes to the wool fibers.

**Vegetal Dyes:**
**Indigo** is a plant *Indigofera tinctoria* that from which the natural vegetal color blue is derived from. Growing wild in many parts of the world the color occurs when the yellow juice of these plants is oxidized.

**Madder** or *Rubia tinctorum* is a perennial herb which is native to the Mediterranean and Near East its roots being a source of red dye. Today with the resurgence in vegetal dyed rugs it has made a striking comeback and is widely grown.

**Pomegranate** or *Punica granatum* is used as a vegetal dye source, depending on the mordant used the color derived is a yellow brownish or black brownish shade. When used as a rug design the fruit represents fertility and abundance due to the many seeds it contains.

**Rhubarb** or *Rumex htmenosepalusor* found throughout many rug producing regions of the world is used as a vegetal dye source and creates a yellow to copper-red color depending on the mordant used.

**Saffron** or *Crocus sativus* was used by the ancient Greeks and Romans as a royal dye source as well as an aromatic perfume. From the 14th thru 18th centuries it was a vegetal dye source for the color yellow in rug production. Known and associated with wealth it requires around 5000 blooms to produce one ounce or so of dye.

**Tumeric** or *Curcuma longa* is one of the most common tropical plants used to derive a yellow vegetal dye color. A cultivated native plant to India, it is also used as a popular spice.

**Aniline dye:** is a synthetic dye that was invented around the year 1900 and is made with a coal tar base.

**Antique wash** is a modern method of antiquing contemporary rugs. By doing this the rug colors are made softer resulting in a used or antique look. The majority of the rugs made using this method are less durable being the result of the harsh chemicals stripping away the natural lanolin found in wool.

Then the wool is rinsed and carefully dried.

Drying wool yarn that has been dyed, Peshawar, Pakistan.

An outdoor work area, Peshawar, Pakistan.

Retrieving well water to use in the dyeing process, Peshawar, Pakistan.

Most dyes today used in the market place are chrome dyes of Swiss origin and have been around since the early 1950s, prior to that much harsher chemical dyes were the norm, which often resulted in the running of colors and actual corrosion of the wool itself. These new chrome dyes utilize potassium di-chromate, which helps the color adhere to the wool and give a very strong pleasing effect in the end product. Vegetal dyes have resurfaced in the last decade as a strong influence in the market place using a variety of natural color sources such as madder root used to produce the color red and the indigo plant for the color blue. As a rule of thumb, the vegetal dyed carpet colors are significantly softer in color than the chrome dyes and with time, they obtain a warm soft patina. A lot of emphasis in the market place has been placed on the value of buying a vegetal dyed rug over a chrome dye, but in reality both, if taken care of properly, will last more than a lifetime.

Completed skeins of dyed wool yarn, Peshawar, Pakistan.

Completed skeins of dyed wool yarn, Peshawar, Pakistan.

The next step in the weaving process is a foundation for the rug, consisting of warps of cotton threads, wool, or silk, which run the length of the rug and wefts of similar threads which pass under and over the warp from one side to the other on the loom. The loom is critical - although they vary in size and sophistication. It is necessary with all looms that the proper tension is used in order to create a finished product that is as perfect as possible.

Although there are various types of looms used today, the vertical loom is most widely encountered and the most comfortable to operate. These looms are found more frequently in city situations, as they are hard to dismantle and transport. Horizontal looms are usually used by more remote village people and they restrict the size of the finished product.

Once set up, the weaving begins by normally passing a number of wefts through the bottom warp to form a base on which to start from. Once started knots of the dyed yarn are then tied around consecutive sets of adjacent warps to create the intricate patterns of the rugs.

Drying wool yarn that has been dyed, Peshawar, Pakistan.

**Foundation** is the basis for a rug with the warp and weft strands on which the knots of the pile are woven into.

A weaver working at a loom, Lahore, Pakistan.

10

Weavers working on looms,
Lahore, Pakistan.

11

Often, the patterns are drawn out by the artisans on paper, as a "cartoon" to follow when weaving.

**Cartoon** is a colored drawing of the intended rug to be produced and is used by the weaver as a guide in color and design.

Coloring and drawing rug cartoons, Lahore, Pakistan.

**Border** is the outside area of the rug acting much like a picture frame to the field of a rug.

**Field** is the largest area in a rug and is enclosed by borders.

As more rows are tied to this foundation, these knots become the pile of the rug. Between each row of knots, one or more passes of weft are used to tightly pack down and secure the rows. Depending on the desired product and materials, and the expertise of the weavers, the knot count can vary anywhere from around 20 or so knots per square inch to as much as 550 knots.

As far as large knot counts determining quality rug, this is a fallacy that perpetrates through the rug trade and is an old "Persian Myth" to justify high prices. Yes, it is true that the more knot count generally indicates a higher clarity in pattern, but if the dyes and designs are not harmonious in their interplay, then it is of no real consequence and poor quality is the end result. Also, due to the physics involved in higher knot counts, the resulting product is thinner. If a thin ply of wool or the like is used, it along with other factors can result in a poor foundation and pile with less durability than the heavier pieces with far less knotting. Also, higher knot counts are usually found in formal city patterns, such as the Sarouk, Tabriz, Kermans, and Kashans etc., and far fewer knots usually are found in the more tribal or village productions found in the market place. It is interesting to note that some of the most expensive antique rugs ever sold by the world's two leading auction houses have had less than 100 knots per square inch.

A weaver with his rug cartoon working at his loom, Lahore, Pakistan.

A weaver at her vertical loom, Lahore, Pakistan.

Working at a floor loom, Lahore, Pakistan.

Another vertical loom, Lahore, Pakistan.

Once the knotting is completed the warp ends form the fringes, which may be weft faced, braided, knotted, etc. and have nothing in reality to do with the finished quality of the carpet itself.

> **Fringes** are part of the foundation of a rug and are basically warps which extend out at the end. In cheap machine made and tufted copies primarily from China artificial fringe is actually sewn to the back of the rug attempting to give it a handmade look.

Many tools are used in rug production, from a comb like instrument for packing down the wefts to large shears for trimming the pile. Once the carpet is removed from the loom it is these tools that are used to uniformly shear the pile to its desired height, often over a wood or metal rod to help maintain a consistent even surface.

Clipping or shearing a completed rug, Lahore, Pakistan.

Tying off the fringe, Lahore, Pakistan.

Making the fringe even. Lahore, Pakistan.

Once completed, the rug is checked by hand for any loose yarns sticking up, Lahore, Pakistan.

Once finished with this last "haircut," the rug is thoroughly washed and dried in the sun to help set the colors.

Burning off excess yarn, Lahore, Pakistan.

Tools of the trade for washing a completed rug, Lahore, Pakistan.

Washing the completed rug, Lahore, Pakistan.

In most cases, due to the current market demands, the rugs are next "sized" or "blocked" by nailing them to wood boards to assure as straight an edge as possible.

**Blocking** is one of the final steps in rug production when the completed rug is immersed in water and then tacked down using small brads or nails to a wood board to get the rug as properly shaped as possible, then allowing the rug to dry.

Removing tacks after the rug has been sized, Lahore, Pakistan.

Tacking down the rug for sizing, Lahore, Pakistan.

Ironing the rug, Lahore, Pakistan.

Ironing the completed rug, Lahore, Pakistan.

When completed, these rugs are sold to individual dealers or, in most cases, to large importers from New York, London, and Zurich, who more than likely "consign" the goods to small retailers or department stores.

Carrying Turkoman rugs to the marketplace, Lahore, Pakistan.

Taking the rug to market, Lahore, Pakistan.

Bailing the rugs for export, Lahore, Pakistan.

Rolling the rug for bailing, Lahore, Pakistan.

Due to the buying power of the large rug importers, the market —although one of individual artistic craftsmanship— is a monopoly controlled by less than twenty major players in the world. Because of this situation, it is difficult for independent retailers to go overseas to successfully buy rugs, although, with a bit of endurance and savvy, it is possible.

It is most advisable *not* to buy a rug overseas while on business or vacation, as you will be greeted by salesmen of unbelievable talent who will lure you into buying a rug at a greatly inflated price, as this is the current state of affairs. You will have the underlying thought that because you are overseas, it must be a great value.

One of the most recent ploys that we have encountered, due to the current war in Iraq and Afghanistan, is the amount of American servicemen, especially in Saudi Arabia, who have purchased rugs, supposedly made in the holy cities of Mecca and Medina, at greatly inflated prices. Only when they return to the United States do they find out their silk rug was in reality mercerized cotton and not made in Saudi Arabia (as they do not traditionally make rugs), and actually a rather poorly made rug of Indian or Chinese origin.

---

**Chemical wash** is a harsh method of producing overall luster on a rug and in the process damaging many of the natural qualities found in wool.

---

**Burn test** is often a method used to test the carpets fiber for content. Silk smells distinctly like human hair when burned, cotton like a vegetable smell, and wool smelling faintly of human hair.

---

When buying a rug in the West, it is best to buy from a *long established retailer* who will warranty the product and stand behind it. One of the many ploys in the trade today is the "trial" of a carpet for a certain amount of time, which is often combined with the statement that they will refund the purchase price at any time the customer would like, if not completely satisfied. In the case of a trial, it allows the retailer to mark up the goods considerably so the merchant is only too happy to accommodate for this so called "service." There is nothing wrong with exchanging a rug within thirty days, for another rug of equal or more value, but the trial is just a marketing ploy used to bring a false sense of security into the game and is often used to justify inflated markups.

Potential customers buy into this, with the comment the rugs look different when they get them home. Rugs should not look different, unless the unscrupulous dealer is using jeweler's lights to make wool look like silk, which is a problem. Keep in mind, rugs are art for the floor and you don't buy a painting or other piece of individual artistic endeavor to match the sofa. But, as most Americans grew up with wall-to-wall carpet, they tend to over compensate when buying a rug that will match all the colors in their entirety, which is the wrong way to go about it. You want just a harmonious look and nothing more. The full money back guarantee at anytime that is claimed by many dealers is also nothing more than a pyramid scheme. Since many retailers change their name and location every few years, it's an easy scam to perpetuate.

**Interior Decorators**

It is my feeling that the need to use an interior decorator is a common fallacy when buying an Oriental rug. After all, they are not living in your home, you are. We find that people use interior decorators as a type of vanity situation, such as is prevalent in the art world today, with the vast array of art consultants running around. It's been my experience that the majority of these decorators are truly only interested in putting their clients into an expensive as possible product so their commission is greater. A good interior decorator will charge only by the hour and never take a cut from the product being sold. In fact, we have had situations where the decorator says that their client will not be buying the product unless we guarantee a large commission to them. They request a check made out to themselves or their company. We do not believe this is the proper way to buy a rug. Do you?

**"Going Out of Business Sales"**

Another scam that is prevalent in the industry is the blight of fake "Going Out of Business Sales," or GOBs. This is the case with the "Tent Sales" conducted by major department store chains, a scourge in the marketplace, not to mention the plague of itinerant rug auctions held under so-called "distress" situations and liquidations at various hotels. One of the most recent scams to come to light is the rash of furniture stores who never had rugs as part of their inventory suddenly having a large inventory, especially in "Going Out of Business" situations. In all of these scenarios, the goods being sold are not even owned by the individuals or companies but are put on consignment, complete with "formula" pricing, where they mark the items up and then give unrealistic markdowns, such as eighty percent or more. Keep in mind, rugs are a commodity and in the wholesale marketplace they have a fixed price which can readily be used as a type of currency. In true fact, these scenarios only work because a greedy and dishonest vendor is trying to take advantage of a consumer. It also requires a consumer who thinks they are getting something for nothing. As I always say, it takes two to play this game. If you think you are getting something for nothing, then look out. In the case of GOBs, there is usually extensive media used to pull in customers, followed usually by an auction, only to find the perpetrator under a new name and store, often in the same neighborhood a short time later. If you see such situations going on, it is wise to report them to your local attorney general's office for further investigation.

Due to the information age we live in and globalization of the world, rugs are truly one of the last bastions for a truly handmade product that, if cared for properly, will last for generations to come. When you think that, in this ever-changing world, you can still find such an art form where a room-size carpet can often take up to a year to produce, it is only too clear that this cottage industry will soon disappear as we know it today in just a few years.

In regard to the Child Labor issue, this is another area where there is a great deal of misinformation forwarded to the public. In the thirty years I have been in this business, I can honestly state that I have never seen very young children knotting a rug. Lets face it, anyone who has a young child can understand that it takes considerable concentration and skill to make a carpet, and young children under the age of ten simply do not for the most part have these capabilities. Children are often seen at looms, sitting alongside their parents, but this due to the fact that there is no readily available daycare and children are brought to the job, adding a muddled confusion to the outside world. It is a good idea, though, to ask your retailer whether or not they certify their rugs as "child labor free." Several organizations in the last few years have sprung up, due to the increased media attention, that certify, under close guidance with local authorities, that indeed their product is child labor free.

"Rug Mark" is the largest organization to certify goods being exported.

Local village children, Peshawar, Pakistan.

As for wages earned by the carpet weaver, they should be looked at in comparison to the overall actual cost of living in the country of origin. With wages rising worldwide, it is a truly remarkable fact that a room size rug can be purchased at all, for such a nominal sum of a couple of thousand dollars (or in many cases even far less) anywhere.

I hope the following pages will help to both inspire and educate you in the selection of your next Oriental rug, and that it adds both comfort and beauty to your home, for the enjoyment of yourself and generations to come.

# helpful hints

## Knot Types

### Ghiordes or Turkish Knot

This type of knot ,which is frequently encountered, is often referred to as the single knot. In a symmetrical knot such as this, the yarn is passed between two adjacent warps, brought back under one, wrapped around both forming a collar, then pulled through the center so that both ends emerge between the two warps.

### Senneh or Persian Knot

Often referred to as the double knot or asymmetrical knot, this one is wrapped around one warp only, then the yarn is passed open behind the adjacent warp so that the two ends are divided by a single warp. It may be open on the left or right; due to this it is often labeled the "asymmetrical" knot.

### Jufti

This knot is tied around four warp strands instead of two. Using this knot vastly reduces the time it takes to weave a rug, and in some cases it is detrimental to the long term strength and durability of the finished product. Also, due to this larger knot size, the clarity in design and pattern suffers.

### Knot Types and Countries of Origin

Rugs using the Senneh and Ghiordes knot are widely employed in the countries of Pakistan, India, Iran, China, Turkey, and Afghanistan. Generally speaking, rugs with curvilinear patterns tend to use the Senneh knot, while rugs with geometric designs use the Ghiordes knot. Caucasian and Anatolian carpets are almost always made using Ghiordes knotting.

### Identifying the Knot Type

The easiest way to determine the type of knot is by examining the back of the rug. If only one bump or loop is visible across the warp where the knot has been tied, then the Senneh knot has been employed. If two bumps are visible, then the Ghiordes knot has most likely been employed. Jufti knotting is evident when comparing the horizontal knot count to the number of warps. If there are more than twice as many warps as there are knots, then this type of knotting was used in construction.

## Standard Rug Sizes

### Standard Rug Sizes In The Market Today

Here is a list of standard rug sizes generally found today. Of course, due to the nature of the product, there may be a wide variation in actual rug sizes, especially those made in villages and by tribal weavers. All sizes listed are in feet.

2 x 3
3 x 5
4 x 6
6 x 9
8 x 10
9 x 12
10 x 14
12 x 15
12 x 18

You will frequently see the larger size listed first in a rug description; this is an ancient ploy used by the very first rug traders to entice the buyer into believing that he or she is getting a larger rug than they actually are. This practice is still prevalent throughout the rug industry today. This practice is another ridiculous result of creative merchandising, often leading to unnecessary confusion.

### Runner sizes

Runners usually start with 6-, 8-, 10-, 12-, 14-, 16-, 18-, and 20-foot lengths, with the majority of the rugs around 30 inches wide. Rugs labeled as "corridor rugs" have much wider widths, 40 to 48 inches wide being the general rule.

### Dining Rooms

One of the most frequently asked questions encountered is "how large a rug is needed under a dining room table?" The following list has proven true in virtually all cases. These sizes allow the chairs around the table to remain on the rug, not half off and half on. By applying this list, room is also provided for serving pieces, buffets, cupboards, etc. to remain off the carpet.

| 4 chairs | 6' x 9' size |
|---|---|
| 6 chairs | 8' x 10' size |
| 8 chairs | 8' x 10' size |
| 10 chairs | 9' x 12' size |
| 12 chairs | 10' x 14' size |

### Living Rooms, Dens, and Studies

Depending how much of the area you want to cover, a good and fairly universal size for a seating arrangement is 6' x 9'. If you want a small area rug, you can use one as small as 4' x 6' in front of a sofa. For a large room where you want all the furniture sitting on a rug, a 9' x 12' size carpet or larger may be required. Consult your Oriental rug professional for help in finding the appropriate size.

### Entryways

Another area of great contention, depending on the look you want, is the size of rug for an entryway. The size can vary from as little as 2' x 3' to as large as 6' x 9'. In all my years in business, I would have to say that 4' x 6' is the most universal size used in this area of the house. As a helpful hint, remember that a standard single door is 30" in width, plus frame and casings.

### Bedrooms

Depending on whether you want to sit your bed on top of a large rug or just highlight the room with rugs around the parameter, the size can vary. I have found that two rugs, such as 3' x 5', work well along the sides with 4' x 6' at the foot of a bed. The following list will give you the dimensions of standard beds today. All sizes are in inches.

| Twin | 39 x 75 |
|---|---|
| Full | 54 x 75 |
| Queen | 60 x 80 |
| King | 78 x 80 |
| California King | 72 x 84 |

### Hallways

It has been my experience that most people have a false perception of size when it comes to hallways. They argue that they need a 24" width runner, since their hallway is not very wide. Most hallways encountered are 34" in width and larger, due to the size of the human body.

When looking for that perfect carpet, always measure the room concerned ahead of time and bring the size and any color swatches or paint colors with you when shopping. If you have blueprints, bring them as well; it makes the selection process easier for all parties concerned. Remember that you can never match a color exactly, as all pile rugs have a nap; depending on how you view the rug, there will be a light as well as a dark side of color intensity. Also, don't be swayed by the opinions of the salesman or interior decorator, use your own tastes and judgment to select your carpet; it is not only a functional part of home décor, but also art for the floor.

## Handmade vs. Machine-made Rugs

**Wilton Rugs** are machine-made rugs using Axminster power looms that copied handmade designs. A British production center, the Wilton Company produced handmade rugs for a very short time as well.

**Axminster** is a type of power loom used for making machine-made copies.

Genuine Oriental rugs are not made in Belgium or anywhere else in Western Europe.

In the United States, the major producers of copies of handmade rugs are the firms Wilton©, Karistan©, and Couristan©. They make their rugs on mechanized power looms in a very short period of time. They are often wool blends mixed with man-made fibers. Why a consumer would buy such a product when the genuine article can be purchased for around the same price (or in some cases substantially less) has always boggled my mind. The machine-made rugs, even those at the high end of the market, have a hard time holding up to the durability, warmth, and look of the genuine Oriental rug. Also, for general servicing Oriental rugs are far superior to their copies, if they are properly cared for. All machine-made rugs, no matter what material they are made from (wool, polypropylene, or nylon) have absolutely no inherent resale value.

Handmade rugs, on the other hand, when properly cared for, and when purchased at fair market values will most likely appreciate in value in the long term, especially today when the ever-increasing wealth and prosperity of the countries of origin continue to increase, along with escalating labor and material costs.

## Lighting

One of the customer's biggest concerns is how the rug will look in the home environment. If the rug retailer does not use jeweler's lights, which make wool rugs appear like silk, or florescent lights, which often dull the colors, then the rug should look very similar in the store to the way it will look in a home setting. Of course, if lots of natural light floods the room at home, the rug may appear differently than it did in the showroom. If possible, ask to see the carpet in natural daylight if this is a concern, and be sure to stay away from a showroom with jeweler's lights. Ask the dealer what type of lighting condition the rugs are being shown in. Don't be afraid to ask. An educated and informed consumer is always the friend of a reputable retailer.

## Hand Tufted Rugs

Known in the trade as "cut" goods, hand-tufted rugs have appeared on the scene in the last two decades and been mass-marketed on television shopping channels and big box stores as "handmade" in China and India. These inexpensive and disposable rugs are a plague in the marketplace. They are made using a hand-held tool that punches strands of yarn into a canvas on a frame; the designs being pre-printed onto the canvas. The workers fill in the pattern using this punch tool with the appropriate yarn color, usually completing a room-size rug in a day or two. Once finished, the product is removed from the frame and the back is covered with a gauze fabric which is glued (usually latex) to the back. It is only the glue that holds the carpet pile in place; and within a relatively short period of time the backing disintegrates and the pile is lost. Recently there have been several claims that homeowners have had allergic reactions to the glue backing. Because of the tufting process, no fringe is naturally produced on these rugs so artificial fringe is added by gluing or sewing it to the ends of the rug. Customers are strongly advised to stay away from these floor coverings and stay with hand-knotted goods.

## Silk Rugs

Silk rugs are both exotic and long wearing. Made from the lustrous fiber secreted by the silkworm when spinning a cocoon, silk's main ingredient is fibrorin. Silk has been used for centuries in weaving rugs and garments and many fine examples survive in museums, mosques, and private collections as early as the 16th century onward. An expensive product to produce, silk rugs make up the one area that is most often misrepresented by rug merchants. Perhaps half of the "silk" rugs being offered in the marketplace today are not silk, but rather rayon or mercerized cotton. Often labeled as "artsilk", they are primarily found in the Kashmir part of India and throughout China. When purchasing a true silk rug, always acquire it from a reputable and long-established merchant. Be especially cautious when making a purchase outside United States, at an itinerant auction, or at a so-called "Going Out of Business Sale."

# Oriental Rug Types

## Afghani Rugs

The troubled area of Afghanistan has a rich history of rug production by various tribal peoples of the region. Hearat, located in northwestern Afghanistan and capital of Hearat Province, is located on the rich and fertile Harirud River. The most beautiful of all the ancient cities, Hearat has a settlement history of over 2,500 years, being fought over by successive rulers from Alexander the Great in 330 B.C. to Ahmad Sgah Durrani in 1749. Under the Mongol conqueror Tamerlane, who made it his capital in 1381, it soon became a center of Persian art and learning and a major center for rug production. Today, the Tekkes, as well as members of the Yomud and Saruq tribes, are weaving various designs based on variations of traditional Turkoman patterns, with Tekkes being the most frequently encountered today.

> **Chobi** is a catch-all word used to describe a type of rug from Afghanistan and Pakistan, especially Peshawar, and is a Farsi word meaning wood. Most of the Chobi rugs seen today are geometric designs in a light brown color.
>
> ---
>
> **Ersari** is a large tribal group of people, mostly settled in northwest Afghanistan, who make both city and tribal rugs.

Another major tribal group producing carpets are the nomadic Baluch, who are located in the areas west and southwest of Hearat along the Iranian border. Today they produce a wide variety of rugs with one of the most distinguishing characteristics being that they are made entirely of wool and are woven on horizontal looms by women only. One of their most famous recent productions for the marketplace has been the introduction of commemorative "War Rugs," depicting the recent conflicts in the country and the events of the 9/11 attacks in New York City.

A major rug type in Afghanistan is the well-known Maimana carpet, from the westernmost province of Afghan Turkestan. These are made by the Uzbek people who produce finely woven kilims, which are always identified by their large amount of yellow and gold colors. Because it is not possible to describe and properly identify in a short clause the vast tribal areas of rug production, we have limited this selectlion to the most commonly seen rugs in today's marketplace.

### The Values of Afghani Rugs Today

#### Pile Rugs
Baluchi (including war rugs): $7 to $10 per square foot
Teke and other Turkomans, 80 to 120 knots per square inch: $7 to $10 per square foot.
Teke and Turkomans, 150 to 200 knots per square inch: $12 to $16 per square foot.
Teke and Turkomans, 225 to 300 knots per square inch, $20 to $30 per square foot.

#### Flatwoven Rugs
Maimana: $5 to $7 per square foot

*Add a 20% premium for all rugs made with vegetal dyes.*

Baluchi rug, 2'9" x 4'7" Wool on wool, vegetal dyes.

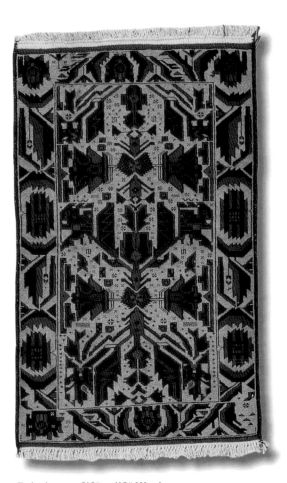

Baluchi rug, 2'9" x 4'3" Wool on wool, Vegetal dyes, Afghanistan.

Baluchi rug, 3' x 4'8" Wool on wool, Chrome dyes, Afghanistan.

Baluchi rug, 2'8" x 4'0" Wool on wool, Chrome dyes, Afghanistan.

Baluchi rug, 3'4" x 6'4"
Wool on wool, Vegetal
dyes, Afghanistan.

Baluchi rug, 3'7" x 5'3" Wool on wool, Chrome dyes,
Afghanistan.

Baluchi rug, 3'4" x 6'2" Wool on
wool, Vegetal dyes, Afghanistan.

Baluchi rug, 3'8" x 6'4" Wool on wool, Vegetal dyes, Afghanistan.

Baluchi rug, 3'8" x 6'9" Wool on wool, Vegetal dyes, Afghanistan.

Baluchi rug, 3'9" x 6'5" Wool on wool, Vegetal dyes, Afghanistan.

Baluchi rug, 4'2" x 6'9" Wool on wool, Vegetal dyes, Afghanistan.

Baluchi rug, 4'8" x 6'4" Wool on wool, Chrome dyes, Afghanistan.

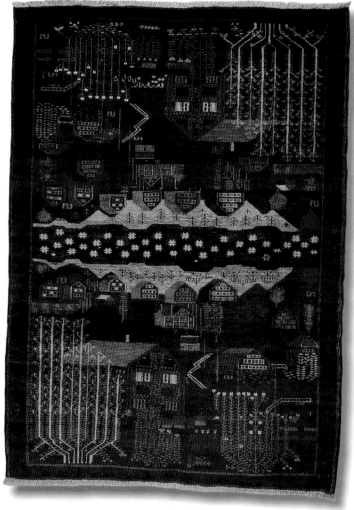

Baluchi rug, 3'2" x 6'0" Wool on wool,
Vegetal dyes, Afghanistan.

Baluchi rug, 3'11" x 6'8" Wool on wool, Vegetal dyes,
Afghanistan.

Baluchi rug, 3'6" x 5'5" Wool on wool,
Chrome dyes, Afghanistan.

Baluchi rug, 3'7" x 6'4"
Wool on wool, Vegetal
dyes, Afghanistan.

Baluchi rug, 3'5" x 6'10" Wool on wool, Chrome dyes,
Afghanistan.

Baluchi rug, 4'5" x 6'2" Wool on
wool, Vegetal dyes, Afghanistan.

Baluchi rug, 3'9" x 5'10" Wool on wool, Chrome dyes, Afghanistan.

Baluchi rug, 3'9" x 6'7" Wool on wool, Chrome dyes, Afghanistan.

Baluchi rug, 4'2" x 5'5" Wool on cotton, Vegetal dyes, Afghanistan.

Baluchi rug, 3'6" x 5'11" Wool on wool, Chrome dyes, Afghanistan.

34

Baluchi rug, 3'8" x 6'1" Wool on wool, Vegetal dyes, Afghanistan.

Baluchi rug, 3'10" x 6'5" Wool on wool, Vegetal dyes, Afghanistan.

Baluchi rug, 3'4" x 5'6" Wool on wool, Chrome dyes, Afghanistan.

Afghani rug, 5'1" x 5'1" Wool on wool,
Vegetal dyes, Afghanistan.

Afghani rug, 5'1" x 5'10" Wool on
wool, Vegetal dyes, Afghanistan.

Afghani rug, 4'10" x 6'4" Wool on wool, Vegetal dyes, Afghanistan.

Balouchi rug, 4'1" x 6'3" Wool on wool, Vegetal dyes, Afghanistan.

Afghani rug, 4'10" x 6'3" Wool on wool, Vegetal dyes, Afghanistan.

Afghani rug, 4'1" x 6'5" Wool on wool, Vegetal dyes, Afghanistan.

Afghani rug, 5'3" x 6'3" Wool on wool, Vegetal dyes, Afghanistan.

Afghani rug, 5'2" x 6'4" Wool on wool, Vegetal dyes, Afghanistan.

Afghani rug, 4'10" x 6'5" Wool on wool, Vegetal dyes, Afghanistan.

**Tekke** is a large Turkoman tribal people that currently inhabit the northeastern part of Iran and nearby Herat, Afghanistan. Known for their Bokhara rugs, the pattern is based on octagonal guls and abstract elephant foot designs. Today most of the Bokhara rugs seen in the marketplace originate in Pakistan.

Afghani rug, 8'9" x 10'2" Wool on wool, Vegetal dyes, Turkoman design.

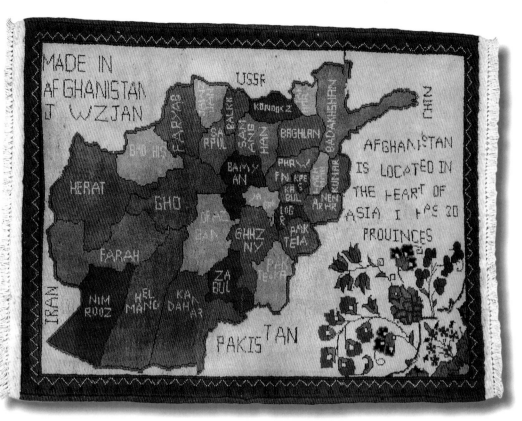

Afghani War rug, 2'2" x 2'0" Wool on wool, Chrome dyes.

Afghani War rug, 2'1" x 2'0" Wool on wool, Chrome dyes.

Afghani War rug, 1'11" x 2'6" Wool on wool, Chrome dyes.

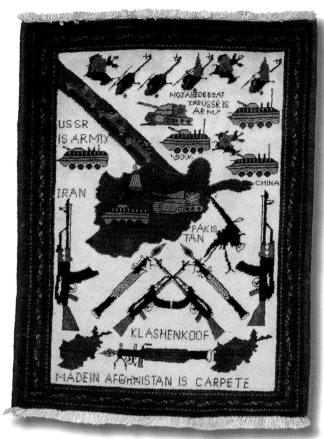

Afghani War rug, 2'0" x 2'8" Wool on wool, Chrome dyes.

Afghani War rug, 1'11" x 2'6" Wool on wool, Chrome dyes.

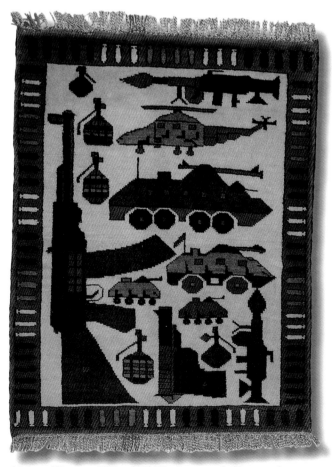

Afghani War rug, 2'0" x 2'5" Wool on wool, Chrome dyes.

Afghani War rug, 2'0" x 2'2" Wool on wool, Chrome dyes.

# Chinese Rugs

Carpet making in China dates back to the Sung Dynasty (960-1279 A.D.). Rugs were produced in workshops controlled by the early emperors, with the designs being characteristic of Buddhism and Taoism. Marco Polo was the first westerner to view these rugs, when he traveled along the Silk Road to China in the 13th century. He was said to be an admirer of these beautiful rugs.

**Soumak** is a flat woven rug that has a embroidery or herringbone effect over the flat surface.

**Aubusson** design carpets were originally made in France from the 15th to 19th centuries drawing their inspiration from royal Moorish artisans. Originally a flat woven rug, today they are made in both India and China in both pile and flat weave versions with the floral center the primary design element.

Today, with China's gross national product growing faster than any other major country in the world, the main areas of rug production are centered on the outskirts of Beijing and Tsing Tao. In the early 1970s, 90-, 160-, 220-, and 300-line carpets were produced and exported to the West. By the 1980s, after trade was opened up with the West, flat woven goods started being produced, such as Kilims, Soumaks, Needlepoints, Aubussons, and Tapestries. All these rugs are currently available from most retailers today. Well known for their dense wool carpets, all-silk rugs are also produced in the more remote smaller villages as well as the two main rug producing cities of Beijing and Tsing Tao.

**Art silk** is short for artificial silk being made from mercerized cotton or in some cases rayon. Found in many rugs from China and Kashmir India it is used to deceive potential buyers.

**Nichols** refers to a rug produced by the Nichols Super Yarn and Carpet Company of Tientsin, China. The firm began business in 1924, and became famous for their "Super Chinese Rug," which was both thick and plush. They had factories in both Shanghai and Peking and supplied their agents and department stores in the West with rugs in their Art Deco designs. Today, the word is synonymous with this type of design. The company ceased operation in the 1930s.

Like silk rugs from India, a large majority of the Chinese so-called silk rugs are actually made of rayon or in some cases mercerized cotton, so it is truly 'buyer beware.' As always, it is best to buy from an established merchant with a good reputation. Remember that there are no "rug police!"

China is unique in their description of knot count by using the term "line". The actual line count measures the number of knots in a linear foot, measured across the width of a rug. For example, in the case of the thick 90 Line carpets, you will find it has 90 knots per linear foot, or 56 knots per square inch. This formula holds true for all Chinese rugs; hence, a 160 Line carpet has around 177 knots per square inch.

The majority of rugs from China are made with chrome dyes.

## The Values of Chinese Rugs Today

### Pile Rugs
90 line (sculptured): $15 to $20 per square foot
160 line (Sino Persian): $25 to $30 per square foot
220 line (Sino Persian): $30 to $35 per square foot
300 line (Sino Persian): $60 to $80 per square foot
(usually silk)

### Flatwoven Rugs
Kilim and Soumak:
$10 to $15 per square foot.
Aubusson, Needlepoint, and Tapestry:
$25 to $30 per square foot

Chinese rug, 2'6" x 8'0" Wool on cotton. 220 line Sino- Persian, Tabriz design.

Chinese rug, 2'6" x 10'0" Wool
on cotton. 220 line Sino Persian,
Tabriz design.

Chinese rug, 6'6" x 6'6"
Wool on cotton. 220 line
Sino Persian, Lavar Ker-
man design.

Chinese rug, 2'3" x 10'0"
Wool on cotton. 220 line
Sino Persian, Kashan
design.

Chinese rug, 6'6" x 6'6"
Wool on cotton. 220 line
Sino Persian, Kerman
design.

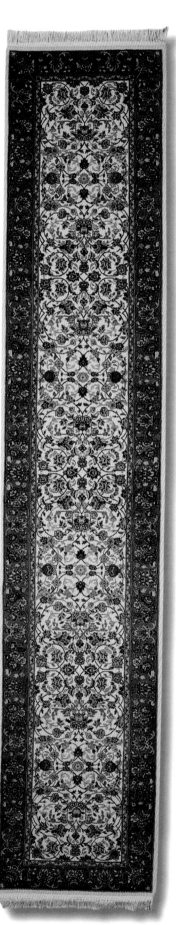

Chinese rug, 2'6" x 12'0" Wool on cotton. 220 line Sino Persian, Kashan design.

Chinese rug, 2'6" x 12'0" Wool on cotton. 220 line Sino Persian, Kashan design.

Chinese rug, 2'6" x 10'0" Wool on cotton. 220 line Sino Persian, Tabriz design.

Chinese rug, 2'6" x 12'0" Wool on cotton. 220 line Sino Persian, Kashan design.

Chinese rug, 2'3" x 11'3" Wool on cotton. 220 line Sino Persian, Tabriz design.

Chinese rug, 2'6" x 10'0" Wool on cotton. 220 line Sino Persian, Tabriz design.

Chinese rug, 3'0" x 5'0" Wool on cotton. 220 line Sino Persian, Kerman design.

Chinese rug, 2'6" x 8'0" Wool on cotton. 220 line Sino Persian, Tabriz design.

Chinese Soumak rug, 7'10" x 9'5" Wool on cotton, Vegetal dyes.

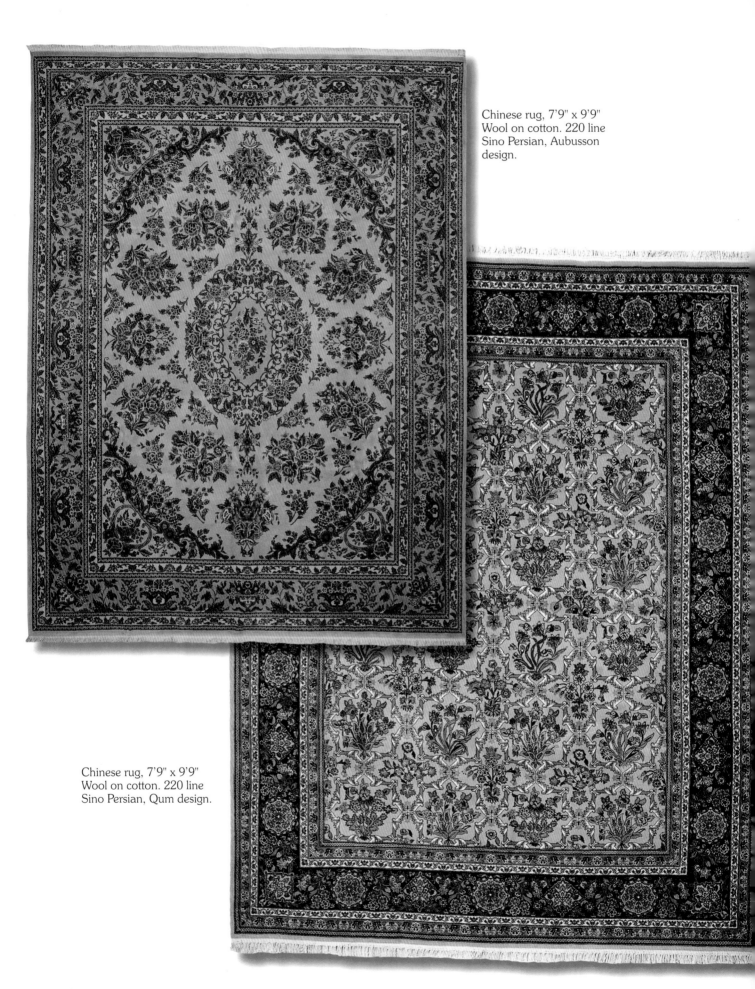

Chinese rug, 7'9" x 9'9"
Wool on cotton. 220 line
Sino Persian, Aubusson
design.

Chinese rug, 7'9" x 9'9"
Wool on cotton. 220 line
Sino Persian, Qum design.

Chinese rug, 8'6" x 11'6" Wool on cotton. 220 line Sino Persian, Kashan design.

Chinese rug, 8'6" x 11'6" Wool on cotton. 220 line Sino Persian, Tabriz design.

49

Chinese rug, 6'0" x 6'0"
Wool on cotton. 220 line
Sino Persian, Kashan design.

Chinese rug, 2'0" x 3'0"
Silk on silk. Hereke
design.

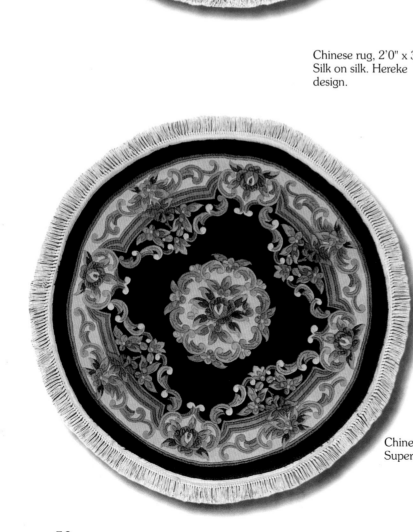

Chinese rug, 6' x 6' Wool on cotton.
Super 90 line Aubusson design.

50

Chinese rug, 2'0" x 3'0" Silk
on silk. Tabriz design.

Chinese rug, 2'0" x 3'0"
Silk on silk. Hereke design.

Aubusson Weave tapestry, 3'2" x 4' 1" Wool on cotton, hand made in China. Based on medieval designs.

Chinese rug, 2'0" x 3'0" Silk on silk. Pictorial design.

Aubusson Weave tapestry, 5'4" x 6' 10" Wool on cotton, hand made in China. Based on 18th century French designs.

Aubusson Weave tapestry, 6'0" x 12' Wool on cotton, hand made in China.
Based on 18th century French  designs.

Aubusson Weave tapestry, 6'3" x 9' 7" Wool on cotton, hand made in
China. Based on 18th century French designs.

Aubusson Weave tapestry, 3'1" x 5' 2"
Wool on cotton, hand made in China.
Based on 18th century French designs.

Aubusson Weave tapestry, 4'2" x 6' 4"
Wool on cotton, hand made in China.
Based on 18th century French designs.

Aubusson Weave tapestry, 6'3" x 9' 2"  Wool on cotton, hand made in China.
Based on 18th century French designs.

Aubusson Weave tapestry, 6'3" x 9' 2"
Wool on cotton, hand made in China.
Based on 18th century French designs.

Chinese needlepoint rug, 6'0" X 9'4"
Wool on cotton. Based on English
designs from the 19th century.

Chinese needlepoint rug, 7'10"
X 9'1" Wool on cotton. Based
on English designs from the 19th
century.

Chinese needlepoint rug, 8' X
10'1" Wool on cotton. Based
on French designs from the 18th
century.

Chinese
needlepoint rug,
8'3" X 10'1"
Wool on cot-
ton. Based on
French Aubus-
son designs
from the 18th
century.

Chinese needlepoint rugs, 8'1" X 10' 100%
Wool. Based on French designs from the
18th century.

Chinese needlepoint rug, 6'2"
X 9'2" Wool on cotton. Based
on French Aubusson designs
from the 18th century.

Chinese needlepoint rug,
7'0" X 10'2" Wool on cotton.
Based on English designs
from the 19th century.

Chinese needlepoint rug, various sizes, Wool on cotton. Based on French and English designs from the 18th and 19th centuries.

Chinese needlepoint rugs,
various sizes, Wool on cotton. Based on French and
English designs from the
18th and 19th centuries.

Chinese needlepoint rug, 8'2"
X 10'2" Wool on cotton. Based
on French designs from the 18th
century.

Chinese needlepoint rug,
7'0" X 10'2" Wool on cotton.
Based on French designs
from the 18th century.

Chinese needlepoint rug,
8'1" X 10'2" Wool on cotton.
Based on French Aubusson
designs from the 18th century.

Chinese needlepoint rug, 8'0" X 10'3" Wool on cotton. Based on French designs from the 18th century.

Chinese needlepoint rug,
8'0" X 10'2" Wool on cotton.
Based on French designs
from the 18<sup>th</sup> century.

Chinese needlepoint rug, 5'0"
X 7'1" Wool on cotton. Based
on French designs from the 18<sup>th</sup>
century.

Chinese needlepoint rug, 6'1"
X 9'5" Wool on cotton. Based
on French designs from the
18<sup>th</sup> century.

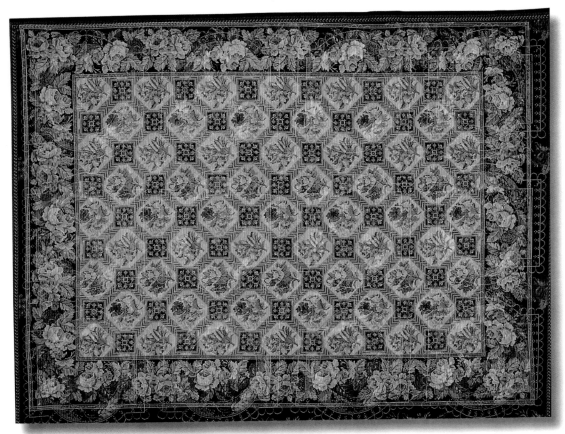

Chinese needlepoint rug, 9'2" X 12'0" Wool on cotton. Based on French designs from the 18th century.

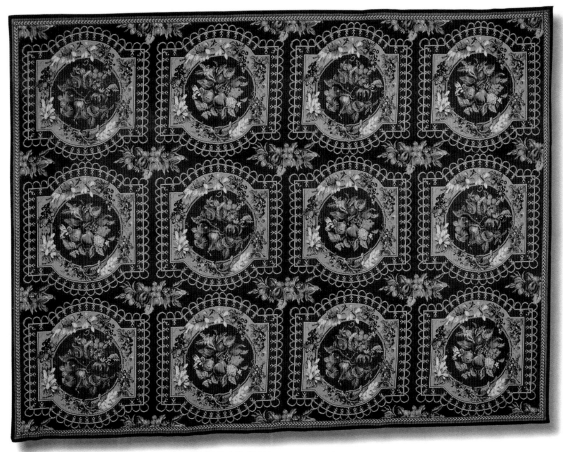

Chinese needlepoint rug, 9'1" X 12'4" Woo on cottonl. Based on English designs from the 19th century.

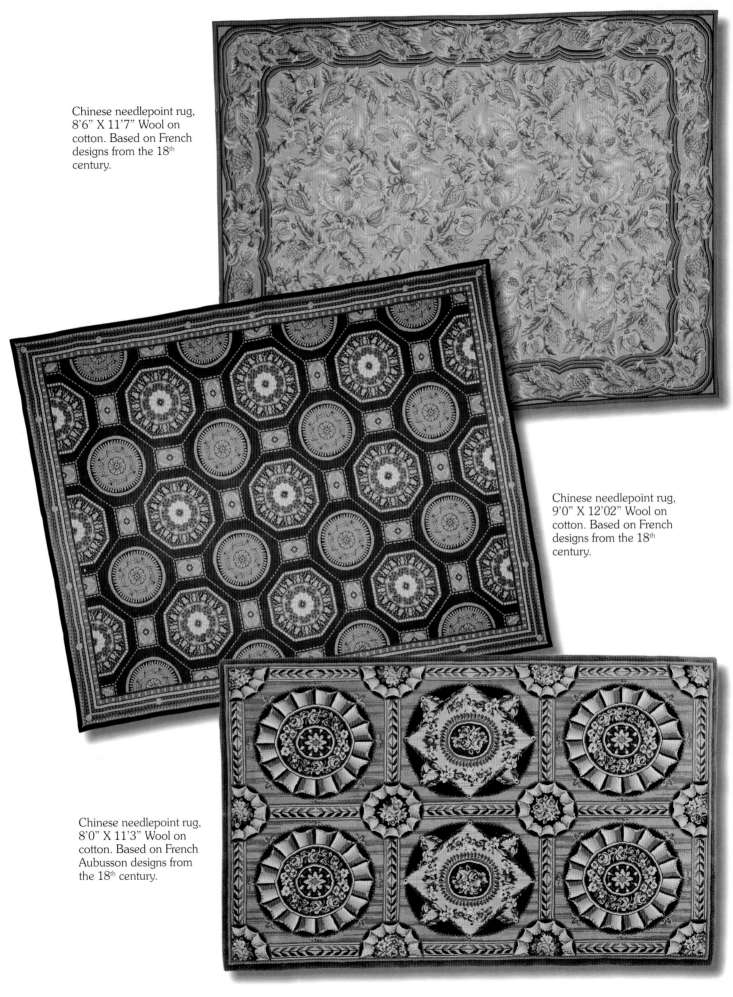

Chinese needlepoint rug, 8'6" X 11'7" Wool on cotton. Based on French designs from the 18th century.

Chinese needlepoint rug, 9'0" X 12'02" Wool on cotton. Based on French designs from the 18th century.

Chinese needlepoint rug, 8'0" X 11'3" Wool on cotton. Based on French Aubusson designs from the 18th century.

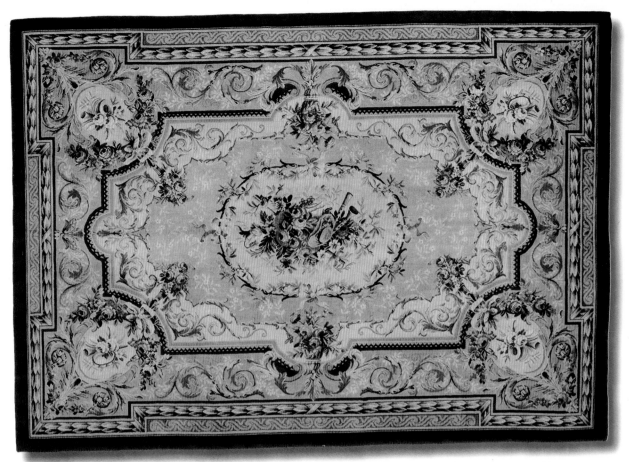

Chinese needlepoint rug, 8'2" X 12'1" Wool on cotton. Based on French Aubusson designs from the 18th century.

Chinese needlepoint rug, 6'0" X 9'3" Wool on cotton. Based on French Aubusson designs from the 18th century.

Chinese needlepoint rug, 9'1" X 11'10" Wool on cotton. Based on French Aubusson designs from the 18th century.

Chinese needlepoint rug, 9'2" X 12'1" Woo on cotton. Based on French Aubusson designs from the 18th century.

Chinese needlepoint rug, 8'0" X 11'7" Wool on cotton. Based on English designs from the 19th century.

Chinese needlepoint rug, 10'0" X 13'9" Wool on cotton. Based on English designs from the 19[h] century.

Chinese needlepoint rug, 7'0" X 9'0" Wool on cotton. Based on French Aubusson designs from the 18th century.

Chinese needlepoint rug, 8'0" X 8'6" Wool on cotton. Based on French Aubusson designs from the 18th century.

Chinese rug, 4'0" x 6'0" Wool on cotton, 220 line Sino Persian, Kashan design.

Chinese needlepoint rug, 5'0" X 8'1" Wool on cotton. Based on French Aubusson designs from the 18th century.

Chinese rug, 3'9" x 5'9" Wool on cotton, 220 line Sino Persian, Kashan design.

Chinese rug, 3'9" x 5'9" Wool on cotton, 220 line Sino Persian, Kashan design.

Chinese rug, 3'9" x 5'9" Wool on cotton, 220 line Sino Persian, Tabriz design.

Chinese rug, 3'2" x 5'1" Wool on cotton, Kashan design, 220 line Sino Persian.

Chinese rug, 3'0" x 5'0"
Wool on cotton, 220 line
Sino Persian, Kashan design.

Chinese rug, 4'0" x 6'0" Wool on cotton, 220 line Sino Persian,
Tabriz design.

Chinese rug, 4'0" x 6'0" Wool
on cotton, 220 line Sino Persian,
Mahi design.

Chinese rug, 4'0" x 6'0"
Wool on cotton, 220
line Sino Persian, Herati
design.

Chinese rug, 4'0" x 6'0" Wool on cotton, 220 line Sino Persian,
Tabriz design.

Chinese rug, 3'9" x 5'9"
Wool on cotton, 220
line Sino Persian, Tabriz
design.

Chinese rug, 3'9" x 5'9" Wool on cotton, 220 line Sino Persian, Kashan design.

Chinese rug, 4'0" x 6'0" Silk on silk, Keyseri design.

Chinese rug, 3'9" x 5'9" Wool on cotton, 220 line Sino Persian, Bakhtiari design.

Chinese rug, 4'0' X 6' 0"
Silk on silk, Hereke design.

Chinese rug, 4'0" x 6'0" Silk
on silk, Keyseri design.

Chinese rug, 2'0" x 3'0" Wool
on cotton, 220 line Sino Persian, Tabriz design.

73

Chinese rug, 2'0" x 3'0" Wool on cotton, 220 line Sino Persian, Kashan design.

Chinese rug, 2'0" x 3'0" Wool on cotton, 220 line Sino Persian, Tabriz design.

Chinese rug, 2'0" x 3'0" Wool on cotton, 220 line Sino Persian, Tabriz design.

Chinese rug, 2'0" x 3'0" Wool on cotton, 220 line Sino Persian, Tabriz design.

74

Chinese rug, 2'0" x 3'0" Wool
on cotton, 220 line Sino Persian,
Tabriz design.

Chinese rug, 3'0" x 5'0"
Silk on silk, Keyseri design.

Chinese rug, 3'0" x 5'0" Silk on silk, Tabriz design.

Chinese rug, 3'0" x 5'0" Silk on silk, Hereke design.

Chinese rug, 3'0" x 5'0" Silk on silk, Hereke design.

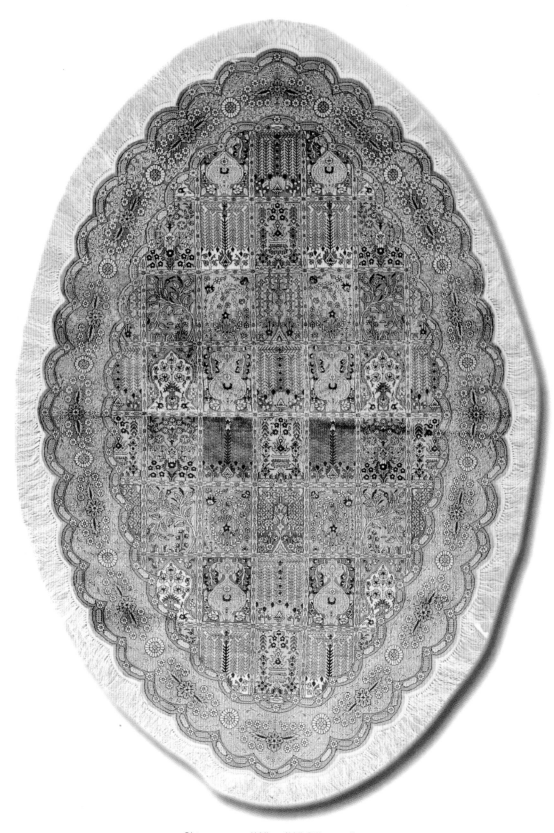

Chinese rug, 4'0" x 6'0" Silk on silk,
Bakhtiari design.

Chinese rug, 4'0" x 6'0" Silk on silk, Keyseri design.

Chinese rug, 4'0" x 6'0"
Silk on silk, Qum design.

Chinese rug, 4'0" x 6'0"
Silk on silk, Hereke design.

# Indian Rugs

The art of carpet making was introduced to India during the reign of Emperor Akbar (1556-1606), ruler of the Moghul Empire in the sixteenth century. Indian workshops under the supervision of master Persian weavers set up production in Lahore (at that time part of the Moghul Empire) producing rugs that were strongly influenced by Persian patterns and designs.

Today, rug production is primarily limited to the two major cities of Varanasi, in east central India, and Jaipur, located near New Delhi.

---

**Jaipur** today is synonymous with a commercial Persian design carpet made in the same region as the area in India that carries its name. Long famous for its rich history of arts and architecture it is one of the major rug producing areas in present day India.

---

**Agra** is a word widely used today to describe a rug made originally by prison labor in the 18th century, in the city by the same name. Agra is home to the Taj Mahal and was seat to the great Moghul ruler Akbar the Great (1556-1606). The pattern is curvilinear in design, drawing inspiration from floral elements. Most Agra carpets today are produced using vegetal dyes, but recently there has been an increasing amount of cheap latex copies flooding the market that should be looked at in one word: disposable.

---

**Dhurrie** is a flat woven wool or cotton rug originating in India. Long popular in the 1980s and early 1990s they were a favorite with interior decorators adding a casual light airy feel to a room.

---

India produces a wide variety of rugs today, with Persian designs and Agra patterns being the most popular. Flatwoven rugs, such as Dhurries, are also woven. The disputed region of Kashmir also produces a small variety of Persian rugs along with "art" (artificial) silk rugs made from mercerized cotton.

---

**Endless knot** is a Buddhist emblem symbolizing long life and duration. Overlapping without a beginning or end it is often used with other symbols to represent the infinite wisdom of nature.

---

**Arabesque design** is a design composed of both linear and intertwined geometric and floral elements.

---

**Directional rug** is a rug with a one way design element and is meant to be viewed from a particular view point such as in a prayer rug.

---

**All-over pattern** refers to carpets that do not possess a center medallion or focal point.

---

The country produces a wide spectrum of qualities, from very low-grade goods made for catalogue sales to very fine hand-knotted masterpieces. Recently, Tibetan patterns have also been introduced in India, but they cannot compare in quality and appearance to their genuine Tibetan counterparts.

## Rug Pricing

### Pile Rugs
9/9 [approx. 81 knots/sq."] (Indo Persian and Agra): $15 to $18 per square foot
10/14 [approx. 140 knots/sq."] (Indo Persian and Agra): $25 to $30 per square foot
13/13 [approx. 169 knots/sq."] (Indo Persian and Agra): $30 to 35 per square foot

Add a 20% premium for rugs made with vegetal dyes.

### Flatwoven Rugs
Dhurrie Rugs, most often encountered in 5 ply 60 count quality: $4 to $6 per square foot

Agra rug, India. 4'3" x 6'1" Wool on cotton, Vegetal dyes, walnut wash. Recreation of 18th century designs.

Agra rug, India. 4'2" x 6'2" Wool on cotton, Vegetal dyes, walnut wash. Recreation of 18th century designs.

Agra rug, India. 4'1" x 6'3" Wool on cotton, Vegetal dyes, walnut wash. Recreation of 18th century designs.

Agra rug, India. 4'2" x 6'6" Wool on cotton, Vegetal dyes, walnut wash. Recreation of 18th century designs.

Agra rug, India. 4'1" x 6'4" Wool on cotton, Vegetal dyes, walnut wash. Recreation of 18th century designs.

Agra rug, India. 4'2" x 6'3" Wool on cotton, Vegetal dyes, walnut wash. Recreation of 18th century designs.

Agra rug, India. 4'1" x 6'2" Wool on cotton, Vegetal dyes, walnut wash. Recreation of 18th century designs.

Agra rug, India. 4'1" x 6'2" Wool on cotton, Vegetal dyes, walnut wash. Recreation of 18th century designs.

Agra rug, India. 4'1" x 5'10" Wool on cotton, Vegetal dyes, walnut wash. Recreation of 18th century designs.

Agra rug, India. 3'10" x 6'3" Wool on cotton, Vegetal dyes, walnut wash. Recreation of 18th century designs.

Agra rug, India. 4'1" x 6'1" Wool on cotton, Vegetal dyes, walnut wash. Recreation of 18th century designs.

Agra rug, India. 4'2" x 6'2" Wool on cotton, Vegetal dyes, walnut wash. Recreation of 18th century designs.

Agra rug, India. 4'1" x 6'3" Wool on cotton, Vegetal dyes, walnut wash. Recreation of 18th century designs.

Agra rug, India. 4'2" x 6'3" Wool on cotton, Vegetal dyes, walnut wash. Recreation of 18th century designs.

Agra rug, India. 4'1" x 6'7" Wool on cotton, Vegetal dyes, walnut wash. Recreation of 18th century designs.

Agra rug, India. 4'1" x 5'10" Wool on cotton, Vegetal dyes, walnut wash. Recreation of 18th century designs.

Agra rug, India. 4'1" x 6'3"
Wool on cotton, Vegetal
dyes, walnut wash. Recreation of 18th century designs.

Agra rug, India. 4'2" x 6'2"
Wool on cotton, Vegetal dyes,
walnut wash. Recreation of
18th century designs.

Agra rug, India. 8'3" x 10'2"
Wool on cotton, Vegetal dyes,
walnut wash. Recreation of
18th century designs.

Agra rug, India. 8'2" x 9'7" Wool
on cotton, Vegetal dyes, walnut
wash. Recreation of 18th century
designs.

Agra rug, India. 8'1" x 10'1"
Wool on cotton, Vegetal dyes,
walnut wash. Recreation of
18th century designs.

Agra rug, India. 8'2" x 10'1"
Wool on cotton, Vegetal dyes,
walnut wash. Recreation of
18th century designs.

Agra rug, India. 8'1" x 10'1" Wool on cotton, Vegetal dyes, walnut wash. Recreation of 18th century designs.

Agra rug, India. 8'2" x 9'10" Wool on cotton, Vegetal dyes, walnut wash. Recreation of 18th century designs.

Agra rug, India.
8'3" x 10'2" Wool
on cotton, Vegetal
dyes, walnut wash.
Recreation of 18th
century designs.

Agra rug, India. 7'10" x 10'1"
Wool on cotton, Vegetal dyes,
walnut wash. Recreation of
18th century designs.

90

Agra rug, India. 8'3" x
10'2" Wool on cotton,
Vegetal dyes, walnut wash.
Recreation of 18th century
designs.

Agra rug, India. 7'10" x 10'1"
Wool on cotton, Vegetal dyes,
walnut wash. Recreation of
18th century designs.

Agra rug, India. 8'0" x 10'1"
Wool on cotton, Vegetal dyes,
walnut wash. Recreation of 18th
century designs.

Agra rug, India. 8'2" x 9'6" Wool on cotton,
Vegetal dyes, walnut wash. Recreation of 18th
century designs.

Agra rug, India. 8'2" x 10'1" Wool
on cotton, Vegetal dyes, walnut wash.
Recreation of 18th century designs.

Agra rug, India. 8'3" x 10'3" Wool on cotton, Vegetal dyes, walnut wash. Recreation of 18th century designs.

Agra rug, India. 8'1" x 10'1" Wool on cotton, Vegetal dyes, walnut wash. Recreation of 18th century designs.

Agra rug, India. 7'10" x 9'10" Wool on cotton, Vegetal dyes, walnut wash. 18th century French-inspired design with Persian elements.

93

Agra rug, India. 8'1" x 10'2"
Wool on cotton, Vegetal dyes,
walnut wash. Recreation of 18th
century designs.

Agra rug, India. 8'1" x
10'3" Wool on cotton,
Vegetal dyes, walnut
wash. Recreation
of 18th century
designs.

Agra rug, India. 8'1" x 10'4" Wool
on cotton, Vegetal dyes, walnut wash.
Recreation of 18th century designs.

Agra rug, India. 8'2" x
10'4" Wool on cotton,
Vegetal dyes, walnut
wash. Recreation of
18th century designs.

Agra rug, India. 8'2" x 10'1"
Wool on cotton, Vegetal dyes,
walnut wash. Recreation of
18th century designs.

Agra rug, India. 7'10" x 9'10" Wool on cotton, Vegetal dyes, walnut wash. Recreation of 18th century designs.

Agra rug, India. 8'1" x 10'1" Wool on cotton, Vegetal dyes, walnut wash. Recreation of 18th century designs.

Agra rug, India. 8'1" x 9'10" Wool on cotton, Vegetal dyes, walnut wash. Recreation of 18th century designs.

Agra rug, India. 8'5" x 9'10"
Wool on cotton, Vegetal dyes,
walnut wash. Recreation of
18th century designs.

Agra rug, India. 8'2" x 11'1"
Wool on cotton, Vegetal dyes,
walnut wash. Recreation of
18th century designs.

Agra rug, India. 8'1" x 10'1"
Wool on cotton, Vegetal dyes,
walnut wash. Recreation of 18th
century designs.

Agra rug, India. 8'9" x 10'10"
Wool on cotton, Vegetal dyes,
walnut wash. Recreation of 18th
century designs.

Agra rug, India. 8'1" x 10'4"
Wool on cotton, Vegetal dyes,
walnut wash. Recreation of 18th
century designs.

Agra rug, India. 8'2" x 9'10"
Wool on cotton, Vegetal dyes,
walnut wash. Recreation of 18th
century designs.

99

Agra rug, India. 8'1" x 9'10"
Wool on cotton, Vegetal dyes,
walnut wash. Recreation of 18th
century designs.

Agra rug, India. 8'3" x 10'2" Wool on cotton, Vegetal
dyes, walnut wash. Recreation of 18th century designs.

Agra rug, India. 8'1" x 10'3" Wool
on cotton, Vegetal dyes, walnut
wash. Recreation of 18th century
designs.

100

Agra rug, India. 8'1" x 10'2" Wool on cotton, Vegetal dyes, walnut wash. Recreation of 18th century designs.

Agra rug, India. 8'2" x 10'3"
Wool on cotton, Vegetal dyes,
walnut wash. Recreation of
18th century designs.

Agra rug, India.
8'1" x 9'9" Wool
on cotton, Vegetal
dyes, walnut wash.
Recreation of 18th
century designs.

Indo Persian rug, 8'1" x 9'10"
Wool on cotton. Kashan design.

Agra rug, India. 8'1" x 9'9" Wool on cotton,
Vegetal dyes, walnut wash. Recreation of 18th
century designs.

Indo Persian rug, 8'1" x 10'2"
Wool on cotton. Kashan design.

103

Indo Persian rug, 2'6" x 12'7" Wool on cotton. Shah Abbas design.

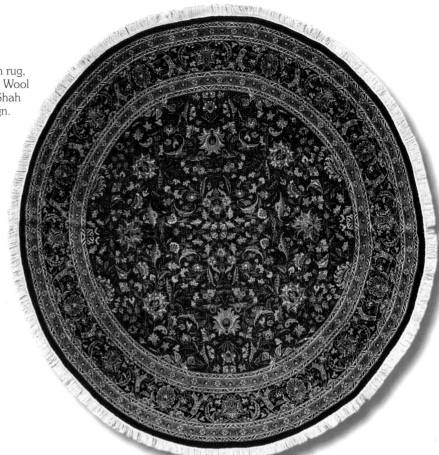

Indo Persian rug, 6'7" x 6'9" Wool on cotton. Kashan design.

Indo Persian rug, 7'2" x 8'10" Wool on cotton. Mahal design.

Indo Persian rug, 8'9" x 9'2" Wool on cotton. Mahal design.

Indo Persian rug, 4'8" x 6'6" Wool on cotton. Shirvan design.

105

Indo Persian rug, 3'0" x 5'3"
Wool on cotton. Tabriz design.

Indo Persian rug, 6'1" x 6'1"
Wool on cotton. Herati design.

Indo Persian rug, 4'0" x 6'0"
Wool on cotton. Tibetan design.

Indo Persian rug, 3'1" x 5'4"
Wool on cotton. Tabriz design.

Indo Persian rug, 2'0" x 5'0" Wool on cotton,
Sarouk design.

Indo Persian rug, 2'10" x 5'0" Wool on cotton,
Avshar design.

Indo Persian rug, 3'1" x 5'5" Wool on cotton, Kashan design.

Indo Persian rug, 3'0" x 5'5" Wool on cotton, Tasbriz design.

Indo Persian rug, 3'2" x 5'0" Wool on cotton, Kashan design.

Indo Persian rug, 3'1" x 5'2" Wool on cotton, Joshagan design.

Indo Persian
rug, 3'2" x 5'3"
Wool on cotton,
Kashan design.

Indo Persian rug,
3'1" x 5'1" Wool
on cotton, Ker-
man design.

Indo Persian rug,
3'2" x 5'5" Wool
on cotton, Herati
design.

Indo Persian rug, 3'1" x 5'1" Wool on cotton,
Kashan design.

Indo Persian rug, 3'1" x 5'2" Wool on cotton,
Kashan design.

# Pakistani Rugs

Partitioned in 1947 from India, Pakistan has a rich and vibrant heritage of rug production, beginning under the Moghul emperor Akbar (1556-1606). In his official history written by his chief minister Abul - Fazl (1551-1602), we have one of the earliest accounts of rug production in the area, "...has caused carpets to be made of wonderful varieties and charming textures, he has appointed experienced workmen who have produced many masterpieces. The carpets of Iran and Turkestan are no more thought of, although some merchants still import carpets from Kirman and Sabzwar. All kinds of carpet - weavers have settled here and drive a flourishing trade. These are found in every town, but especially Agra, Fathpur and Lahore." Still centered in the city of Lahore several centuries later, production was commercialized under the direction of the British East India Company in the seventeenth century, opening the ports to export and encouraging carpet weaving as a cottage industry throughout the subcontinent. After partition in 1947, the weaving, still based in Lahore, was limited to South Kashmiri families from Amritsar, who set up shops in struggling trade to the West.

**Salor** is a Turkoman tribe well known for their fine rugs.

**Hatchlu** is a type of rug or weaving originally used to cover Turkoman tents. The very distinctive pattern is that of a field that is divided into sections by stripes or bar elements as is sometimes seen today in Bokhara rugs from Pakistan.

**Bokhara** is both a city in Uzbekistan and popular pattern based on rows of repeated geometric motifs or Guls said to represent abstract elephant feet.

**Gul** is a term that refers to the octagonal and angular medallions found in Turkoman and Bokhara rugs.

**Mihrab** is a design element most often seen in prayer rugs and represents the prayer point or direction used to face Mecca. The most common motifs seen are arches, points, and blunt ends.

**Palmette** is a design element based on a lotus flower and is found in geometric and curvilinear rugs.

**Rosette** is a commonly used design element representing a rose and is a circular arrangement of motifs radiating out from the center and can be used in various arrangements in a rug design.

Pakistan produces the finest and most consistent quality goods today, from very fine quality Bokhara to superb Persian and Moghul masterpieces, made using innovative dying techniques and fine quality materials, such as New Zealand wool and high-ply cotton. Unlike Iran, whose carpet production incorporates much harsher colors and dyeing techniques and local wool, Pakistani rugs for the most part have a much more harmonious color palette without the use of the electric colors so often encountered in Iranian rugs made in the last 50 years or so.

**Ziegler**, or Mahal, rugs were produced by the German firm of Ziegler and Company of Manchester, England, beginning in the year 1883, after establishing looms under contract in Sultanabad, Iran. Trading in both opium and rugs the firm employed well known designers from such major Western department stores as Liberty of London and B Altman just to name a few. The designs were adapted from 16th and 17th century traditional patterns from the East to fit the conservative demands of the late Victorian world. Well known for using cutting edge and highly developed dying techniques, which they unsuccessfully tried to patent, they employed the best weavers from the region. The rugs were an instant hit with the well-heeled set, especially with Western industrialists due to the softer palettes, which were lacking in their Persian counterparts. The Ziegler designs were composed of rosettes, palmettes, and forked tendrils all intended for this new market. Today Pakistan is the major producer of these beautiful carpets, although it is not unusual to find a Ziegler from India or Turkey as well.

## The Values of Pakistani Rugs Today

The following prices and knot counts are for rugs that are frequently encountered in the current marketplace.

### Pile Rugs
9/9 [approx. 81 knots/sq."] Peshawar and Swat - handspun Afghan wool): $30 to $40 per square foot
12/12 [approx. 144 knots/sq."] (Bokhara and Mori): $10 to $15 per square foot
11/22 [approx. 242 knots/sq."] (Bokhara and Mori): $15 to $20 per square foot
16/16 [approx. 256 knots/sq."] (Persian and Moghul - New Zealand wool): $40 to $50 per square foot
16/18 [approx. 288 knots/sq."] (Persian and Moghul - New Zealand wool): $60 to $75 per square foot
20/20 [approx. 400 knots/sq."] (Persian and Moghul - New Zealand wool): $80 to $100 per square foot

Add a 20% premium for rugs made with vegetal dyes

Pakistani rug, 8'2" x 10'1" New Zealand wool on cotton. 16/18 Quality, Chrome dyes. Northern Pakistan, Nain design.

Pakistani rug, 8'6" x 10'3" New Zealand wool on cotton. Vegetal dyes. Northern Pakistan, Sultanabad design.

Pakistani rug, 7'9" x 10'2" New Zealand wool on cotton, Vegetal dyes. Northern Pakistan, Zeigler design.

111

Pakistani rug, 8'3" x 11' 9" New Zealand wool on cotton, Vegetal dyes. Northern Pakistan, Tree of Life design.

Pakistani Rug, 7'8" x 10'1" New Zealand wool on cotton, Vegetal dyes. Northern Pakistan, Tree of Life design.

Pakistani Rug, 7'11" x 9'10" New Zealand wool on cotton, Vegetal dyes. Northern Pakistan, Aubusson design.

112

Pakistani rug, 8'1" x 10'2" New Zealand wool on cotton, Vegetal dyes. Northern Pakistan, Swat Collection.

Pakistani rug, 8' x 9'11" New Zealand wool on cotton, Vegetal dyes. Northern Pakistan, Zeigler design.

Pakistani rug, 8'1" x 10'5" New Zealand wool on cotton, Vegetal dyes. Northern Pakistan, Mahal design.

Pakistani rug, 8'4" x 10'7"
New Zealand wool on cotton,
16/18 Quality, Vegetal dyes.
Northern Pakistan, Kashan
design.

Pakistani rug, 7'10" x 9'9" New Zealand wool on cotton, Vegetal
dyes. Northern Pakistan, Swat Collection.

Pakistani rug, 8'3" x 10'2" New
Zealand wool on cotton, Vegetal
dyes. Northern Pakistan, Swat
collection.

Pakistani rug, 8'4" x 10'2" New Zealand wool on cotton, Vegetal dyes. Northern Pakistan, Tree of Life design.

Pakistani rug, 9'2" x 12'6" New Zealand wool on cotton, Vegetal dyes. Northern Pakistan Mahal design

Pakistani rug, 6'1" x 9'4" New Zealand
wool on cotton, Vegetal dyes. Northern
Pakistan, Swat collection.

Pakistani rug, 8'4" x 11'7" New
Zealand wool on cotton, Vegetal dyes.
Northern Pakistan, Ziegler design.

Pakistani rug, 6'2" x 8'10" New Zealand wool on cotton. 16/18 quality, chrome dyes.
Northern Pakistan, Isfahan design.

Pakistani rug, 6'1" x 9'3" New Zealand wool on cotton. 16/18 quality, chrome dyes. Northern Pakistan, Tabriz design.

Pakistani rug, 6'2" x 9'4" New Zealand wool on cotton. 16/18 quality, chrome dyes. Northern Pakistan, Bakhtiari design.

Pakistani rug, 6'2" x 8'3" New Zealand wool on cotton. 16/18 quality, chrome dyes. Northern Pakistan, Aubusson design.

Pakistani rug, 6'1" x 9'2" New Zealand wool on cotton. 16/18 quality, chrome dyes. Northern Pakistan, Trellis design.

Pakistani rug, 6'1" x 9'3"
New Zealand wool on cotton.
16/18 quality, chrome dyes.
Northern Pakistan, Tabriz
design.

Pakistani rug, 6'2" x 9'3" New
Zealand wool on cotton. 16/18
quality, chrome dyes. Northern
Pakistan, Sarouk design.

120

Pakistani rug, 6'2" x 8'10" New Zealand wool on cotton. 16/18 quality, chrome dyes. Northern Pakistan, Arles design.

Pakistani rug, 5'10" x 9'3" Vegetaal dyed New Zealand wool on cotton. 16/18 quality. Northern Pakistan, Mughal design.

Pakistani rug, 6'1" x 9'2" New Zealand wool on cotton. 16/18 quality, chrome dyes. Northern Pakistan, Kashan design.

Pakistani rug, 6'0" x 9'5" New Zealand wool on cotton. 16/18 quality, chrome dyes. Northern Pakistan, Arles design.

Pakistani rug, 6'2" x 8'8" New Zealand wool on cotton. 16/18 quality, chrome dyes. Northern Pakistan, Kashan design.

Pakistani rug, 6'2" x 9'1" New Zealand wool on cotton. 16/18 quality, chrome dyes. Northern Pakistan, Arles design.

Pakistani rug, 6'3" x 8'10" New Zealand wool on cotton. 16/18 quality, chrome dyes. Northern Pakistan, Arles design.

Pakistani rug, 6'2" x 9'2" New Zealand wool on cotton. 16/18 quality, chrome dyes. Northern Pakistan, Arles design.

Pakistani rug, 6'2" x 9'2" New Zealand wool on cotton. 16/18 quality, chrome dyes. Northern Pakistan, Bakhtiari design.

123

Pakistani rug, 6'2" x 9'10" New
Zealand wool on cotton. 16/18
quality, chrome dyes. Northern
Pakistan, Aubusson design.

Pakistani rug, 6'1" x 8'10"
New Zealand wool on cotton.
16/18 quality, chrome dyes.
Northern Pakistan, Mughal
design.

Pakistani rug, 6'1" x 9'2" New Zealand wool on cotton. 16/18 quality, chrome dyes. Northern Pakistan, Tabriz design.

Pakistani rug, 6'1" x 8'10" New Zealand wool on cotton. 16/18 quality, chrome dyes. Northern Pakistan, Qum design.

Pakistani rug, 6'2" x 9'5" New Zealand wool on cotton. 16/18 quality, chrome dyes. Northern Pakistan, Tabriz design.

Pakistani rug, 6'2" x 9'1"
New Zealand wool on cotton.
16/18 quality, chrome dyes.
Northern Pakistan, Hunt
scene, Tabriz design.

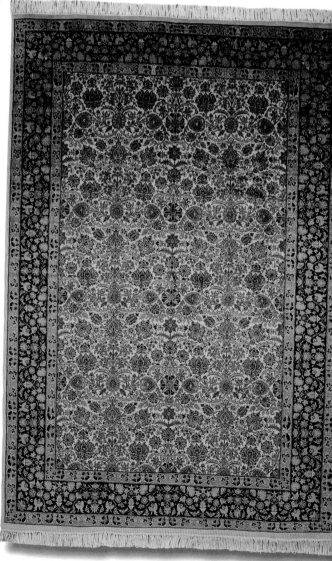

Pakistani rug, 6'3" x 9'2" New
Zealand wool on cotton. 16/18
quality, chrome dyes. Northern
Pakistan, Kashan design.

Pakistani rug, 6'1" x 9'3" New Zealand wool on cotton. 16/18 quality, chrome dyes. Northern Pakistan, Arles design.

Pakistani rug, 6'3" x 9'1" New Zealand wool on cotton. 16/18 quality, chrome dyes. Northern Pakistan, Kashan design.

Pakistani rug, 6'2" x 9'8" New Zealand wool on cotton. 16/18 quality, chrome dyes. Northern Pakistan, Kashan design.

Pakistani rug, 6'1" x 9'1" New
Zealand wool on cotton. 16/18
quality, chrome dyes. Northern
Pakistan, Arles design.

Pakistani rug, 6'1" x 9'4" New Zealand
wool on cotton. 16/18 quality, chrome
dyes. Northern Pakistan, Lavar -Kerman
design.

Pakistani rug, 6'8" x 10'2" New Zealand wool on cotton. 16/18 quality, chrome dyes. Northern Pakistan, Kashan design.

Pakistani rug, 6'3" x 9'2" New Zealand wool on cotton. 16/18 quality, chrome dyes. Northern Pakistan, William Morris design.

129

Pakistani rug, 6'3" x 9'3" New Zealand
wool on cotton. 16/18 quality, chrome dyes.
Northern Pakistan, Aubusson design.

Pakistani rug, 6'2" x 9'1"
New Zealand wool on cotton.
16/18 quality, Vegetal dyes.
Northern Pakistan, Mughal
design.

Pakistani rug, 6'1" x 8'10"
New Zealand wool on cotton.
16/18 quality, chrome dyes.
Northern Pakistan, Kashan
design.

Pakistani rug, 6'2"
x 9'4" New Zealand
wool on cotton. 16/18
quality, chrome dyes.
Northern Pakistan,
Tabriz design.

Pakistani rug, 6'1" x 9'6" New Zealand
wool on cotton. 16/18 quality, chrome
dyes. Northern Pakistan, Qum design.

Pakistani rug, 6'2" x 9'2" New Zealand wool on cotton. 16/18 quality, chrome dyes. Northern Pakistan, Kashan design.

Pakistani rug, 6'1" x 9'2" New Zealand wool on cotton. 16/18 quality, chrome dyes. Northern Pakistan, Mughul design.

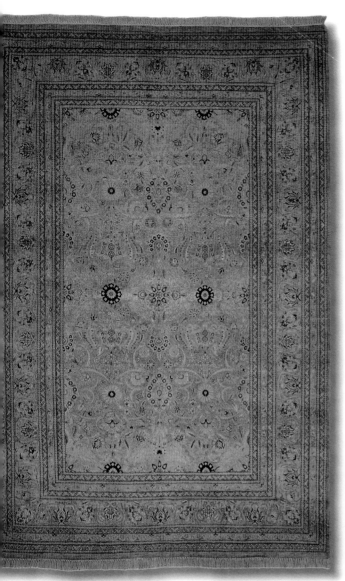

Pakistani rug, 6'1" x 9'3"
New Zealand wool on cotton.
16/18 quality, chrome dyes.
Northern Pakistan, Tabriz
design.

Pakistani rug, 6'4" x 9'6"
New Zealand wool on cotton.
16/18 quality, chrome dyes.
Northern Pakistan, Sultanabad
design.

Pakistani rug, 6'2" x 9'4" New Zealand wool on cotton. 16/18 quality, Vegetal dyes. Northern Pakistan, Moghul design.

Pakistani rug, 3'2" x 5'2" New Zealand wool on cotton. Jaldar design.

Pakistani rug, 3'2" x 5'2" New Zealand wool on cotton. Jaldar design.

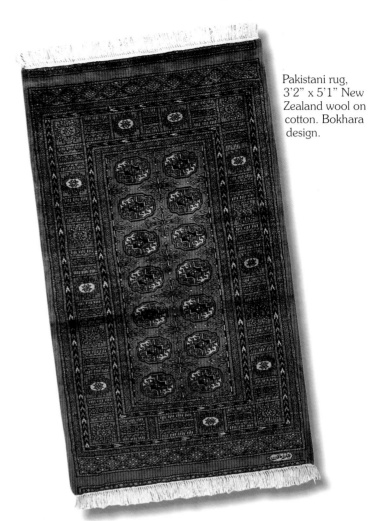

Pakistani rug,
3'2" x 5'1" New
Zealand wool on
cotton. Bokhara
design.

Pakistani rug, 3'2" x 5'3" New Zealand wool on
cotton. Bokhara design.

Pakistani rug,
3'2" x 5'4" New
Zealand wool on
cotton. Bokhara
design.

Pakistani rug, 3'2" x 5'1" New Zealand wool on
cotton. Hatchlou design.

135

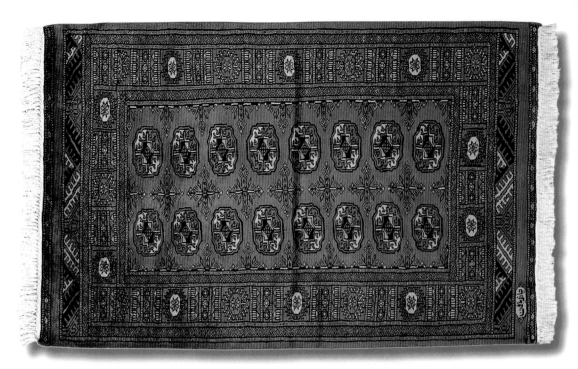

Pakistani rug, 2'11" x 4'8" New Zealand wool on cotton. Bokhara design.

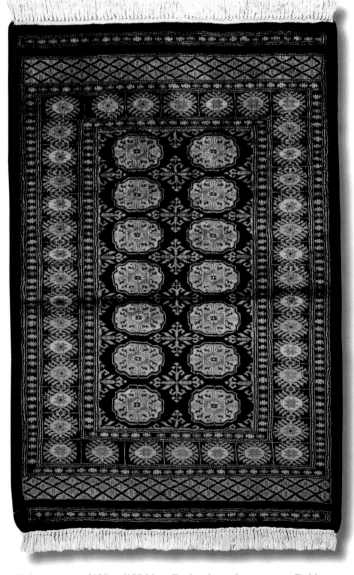

Pakistani rug, 3'1" x 5'5" New Zealand wool on cotton. Bokhara design.

Pakistani rug, 3'2" x 4'8" New Zealand wool on cotton. Bokhara design.

Pakistani rug, 6'1" x 6'6" New Zealand wool on cotton. Bokhara design.

Pakistani rug, 4'2" x 6'5" New Zealand wool on cotton. Bokhara design.

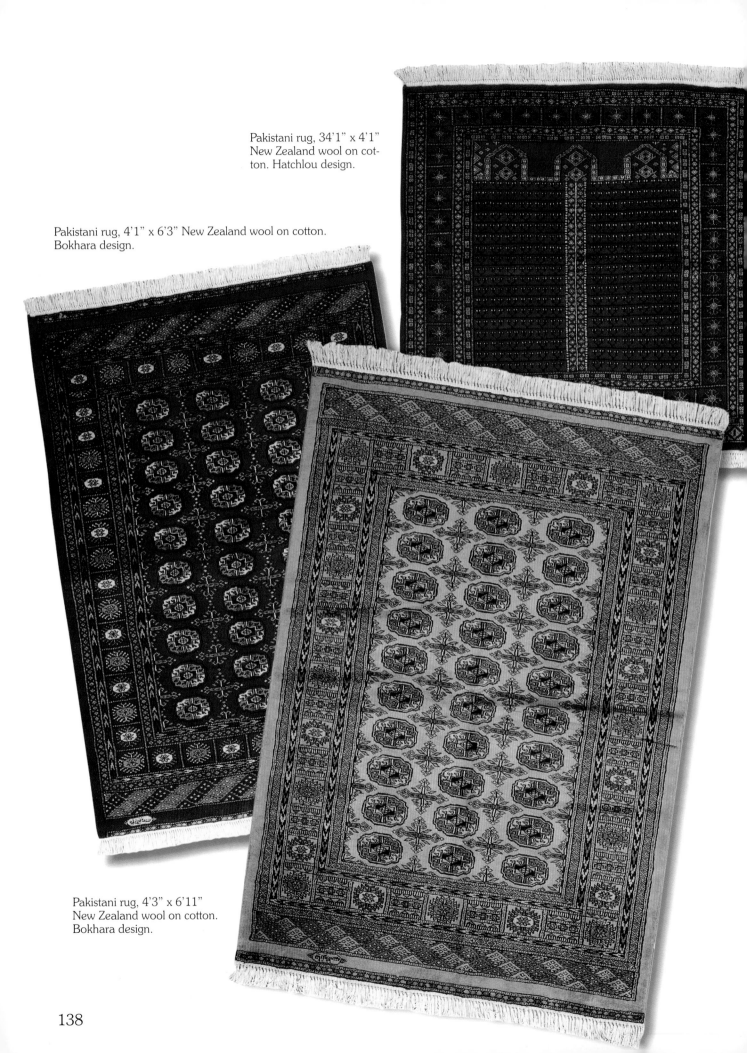

Pakistani rug, 34'1" x 4'1"
New Zealand wool on cotton. Hatchlou design.

Pakistani rug, 4'1" x 6'3" New Zealand wool on cotton.
Bokhara design.

Pakistani rug, 4'3" x 6'11"
New Zealand wool on cotton.
Bokhara design.

138

Swat rug, northern Pakistan, 7'4" x 9'9". Hand spun New Zealand wool on cotton, Vegetal dyes. Designs and motifs loosely based on ancient Caucasian patterns.

Swat rug, northern Pakistan, 7'4" x 9'9". Hand spun New Zealand wool on cotton, Vegetal dyes. Designs and motifs loosely based on ancient Caucasian patterns.

139

Swat rug, northern Pakistan, 7'10" x 9'5". Hand spun New Zealand wool on cotton, Vegetal dyes. Ziegler design.

Swat rug, northern Pakistan, 8'1" x 10'4". Hand spun New Zealand wool on cotton, Vegetal dyes, Sultanabad design.

Swat rug, northern Pakistan, 7'7" x 10'5". Hand spun New Zealand wool on cotton, Vegetal dyes. Designs and motifs loosely based on ancient Caucasian patterns.

Swat rug, northern Pakistan, 8'2" x 10'1". Hand spun New Zealand wool on cotton, Vegetal dyes. Designs and motifs loosely based on ancient Turkish patterns.

141

Swat rug, northern Pakistan, 7'5" x 9'10".
Hand spun New Zealand wool on cotton,
Vegetal dyes. Designs and motifs loosely
based on ancient Persian patterns.

Swat rug, northern Pakistan, 8'2" x 10'10".
Hand spun New Zealand wool on cotton, Vegetal dyes. Designs and motifs loosely based on
ancient Persian patterns.

Swat rug, northern Pakistan, 8'1" x 9'10".
Hand spun New Zealand wool on cotton,
Vegetal dyes. Designs and motifs loosely
based on ancient Caucasian patterns.

142

Swat rug, northern Pakistan, 6'2" x 11'6". Hand spun New Zealand wool on cotton, Vegetal dyes. Designs and motifs loosely based on ancient Caucasian patterns.

Swat rug, northern Pakistan, 4'5" x 5'5". Hand spun New Zealand wool on cotton, Vegetal dyes. Designs and motifs loosely based on ancient Caucasian patterns.

Swat rug, northern Pakistan, 4'5" x 5'10". Hand spun New Zealand wool on cotton, Vegetal dyes. Designs and motifs loosely based on ancient Tribal Persian patterns.

143

Swat rug, northern Pakistan, 4'4" x 5'9". Hand spun New Zealand wool on cotton, Vegetal dyes. Designs and motifs loosely based on ancient Ottoman patterns.

Swat rug, northern Pakistan, 4'2" x 7'1". Hand spun New Zealand wool on cotton, Vegetal dyes. Designs and motifs loosely based on ancient Ottoman patterns.

Swat rug, northern Pakistan, 5'4" x 5'10". Hand spun New Zealand wool on cotton, Vegetal dyes. Designs and motifs loosely based on ancient Chinese patterns.

Swat rug, northern Pakistan, 7'2" x 10'4". Hand spun New Zealand wool on cotton, Vegetal dyes.
Designs and motifs loosely based on ancient Persian Serapi patterns.

Swat rug, northern Pakistan, 7'5" x 10'6". Hand spun New Zealand wool on cotton, Vegetal dyes. Designs and motifs loosely based on ancient Caucasian patterns.

Swat rug, northern Pakistan, 5'8" x 8'7". Hand spun New Zealand wool on cotton, Vegetal dyes. Designs and motifs loosely based on ancient Ottoman patterns.

Swat rug, northern Pakistan, 7'4" x 11'1". Hand spun New Zealand wool on cotton, Vegetal dyes. Designs and motifs loosely based on ancient Persian patterns.

146

Swat rug, northern Pakistan, 6'1" x 8'8".
Hand spun New Zealand wool on cotton,
Vegetal dyes. Designs and motifs loosely
based on ancient Ottoman patterns.

Swat rug, northern Paki-
stan, 8'11" x 11'9". Hand
spun New Zealand wool
on cotton, Vegetal dyes.
Sultanabad design.

Swat rug, northern Pakistan, 7'2" x 9'10".
Hand spun New Zealand wool on cotton,
Vegetal dyes. Designs and motifs loosely
based on ancient Turkish Oushak patterns.

Swat rug, northern Pakistan, 8'2" x 9'10". Hand spun New
Zealand wool on cotton, Vegetal dyes. Designs and motifs
loosely based on ancient Caucasian patterns.

Swat rug, northern Pakistan, 7'4" x 9'9".
Hand spun New Zealand wool on cotton,
Vegetal dyes. Designs and motifs loosely
based on ancient Persian Tabriz patterns.

148

Swat rug, northern Pakistan, 3'10" x 6'1".
Hand spun New Zealand wool on cotton,
Vegetal dyes. Designs and motifs loosely
based on ancient Persian Shirvan patterns.

Swat rug, northern Pakistan, 5'1" x 6'5". Hand spun New Zealand
wool on cotton, Vegetal dyes. Designs and motifs loosely based on
ancient Chinese patterns.

Swat rug, northern Pakistan, 5'3" x 6'5".
Hand spun New Zealand wool on cotton,
Vegetal dyes. Ziegler design.

149

Swat rug, northern Pakistan, 4'10" x 6'4".
Hand spun New Zealand wool on cotton,
Vegetal dyes. Designs and motifs loosely
based on ancient Persian patterns.

Swat rug, northern Pakistan, 6'1" x 9'4". Hand spun New Zealand
wool on cotton, Vegetal dyes. Designs and motifs loosely based on
ancient Ottoman design.

Swat rug, northern Pakistan, 4'2" x 6'2". Hand
spun New Zealand wool on cotton, Vegetal dyes.
Ziegler design.

150

Swat rug, northern Pakistan, 5'7" x 6'10". Hand spun New Zealand wool on cotton,
Vegetal dyes. Designs and motifs loosely based on ancient Caucasian patterns.

Pakistani rug, 3'1" x 5'0" New Zealand
wool on cotton. 16/18 quality, chrome
dyes. Northern Pakistan, Tabriz design.

Pakistani rug, 3'3" x 5'1" New Zealand
wool on cotton. 16/18 quality, chrome
dyes. Northern Pakistan, Tabriz design.

Pakistani rug, 3'2" x 5'5" New Zealand wool on cotton. 16/18 quality, chrome dyes. Northern Pakistan, Arles design.

Swat rug, northern Pakistan, 10'9" x 12'1" New Zealand wool on wool, Vegetal dyes. Designs are motifs loosely based on ancient Persian Serapi designs.

Swat rug, northern Pakistan, 3'4" x 4'10" New Zealand wool on wool, Vegetal dyes. Caucasian design.

Swat rug, northern Pakistan, 3'5" x 5'1" New Zealand wool on wool, Vegetal dyes. Caucasian design.

Swat rug, northern Pakistan, 3'4" x 4'10" New Zealand wool on wool, Vegetal dyes. Persian design.

Swat rug, northern Pakistan, 3'1" x 5'0" New Zealand wool on wool, Vegetal dyes. Caucasian design.

153

Swat rug, northern Pakistan, 8'4" x 11'9" New Zealand wool on wool, Vegetal dyes. Caucasian design.

Swat rug, northern Pakistan, 3'1" x 5'2" New Zealand wool on wool, Vegetal dyes. Bakhtiari design.

Swat rug, northern Pakistan, 8'9" x 11'10" New Zealand wool on wool, Vegetal dyes. Kazak design.

154

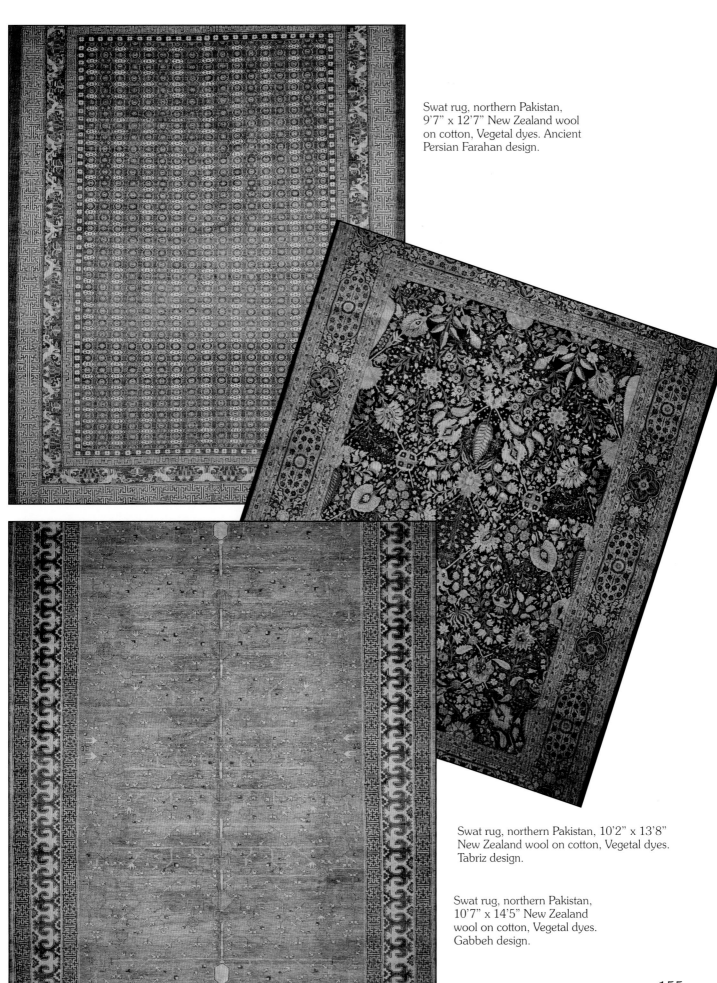

Swat rug, northern Pakistan,
9'7" x 12'7" New Zealand wool
on cotton, Vegetal dyes. Ancient
Persian Farahan design.

Swat rug, northern Pakistan, 10'2" x 13'8"
New Zealand wool on cotton, Vegetal dyes.
Tabriz design.

Swat rug, northern Pakistan,
10'7" x 14'5" New Zealand
wool on cotton, Vegetal dyes.
Gabbeh design.

Swat rug, northern Pakistan,
8'4" x 9'9" New Zealand
wool on cotton, Vegetal dyes.
Tabriz design.

Swat rug, northern Pakistan,
5'8" x 8'5" New Zealand
wool on cotton, Vegetal
dyes. Tabriz design.

156

Swat rug, northern Pakistan, 8'3" x 10'1" New Zealand wool on cotton, Vegetal dyes. Agra design.

Swat rug, northern Pakistan, 7'10" x 9'7" New Zealand wool on cotton, Vegetal dyes. Turkoman design.

Swat rug, northern Pakistan, 8'7" x 9'5" New Zealand wool on cotton, Vegetal dyes. Senneh design.

157

Swat rug, northern Pakistan,
7'8" x 10'3" New Zealand
wool on cotton, Vegetal dyes.
Ottoman design.

Swat rug, north-
ern Pakistan,
5'10" x 8'3"
New Zealand
wool on cotton,
Vegetal dyes.
Persian design.

Swat rug, northern Pakistan,
5'9" x 8'10" New Zealand
wool on cotton, Vegetal dyes.
Designs are motifs loosely
based on antique Caucasian
patterns.

Swat rug, northern
Pakistan,6'6" x 8'10"
New Zealand wool on
cotton, Vegetal dyes.
Vase design.

Swat rug, northern Pakistan,
5'4" x 8'4" New Zealand
wool on cotton, Vegetal dyes.
Serapi design.

Swat rug, northern Pakistan, 5'10" x 8'10"
New Zealand wool on cotton, Vegetal dyes.
Ardebil design.

Swat rug, northern Pakistan, 6'1" x 9'9"
New Zealand wool on cotton, Vegetal
dyes. Caucasian design.

160

Swat rug, northern Pakistan, 5'9" x 7'9"
New Zealand wool on cotton, Vegetal
dyes. Persian design.

Swat rug, northern
Pakistan, 5'7" x 8'6"
New Zealand wool on
cotton, Vegetal dyes.
Caucasian design.

Pakistani rug, 5'1" x 3'2" New Zealand
wool on cotton, 16/18 quality, chrome
dyes. Northern Pakistan, Qum design.

Swat rug, northern Pakistan, 4'5" x 5'3"
New Zealand wool on cotton, Vegetal dyes.
Caucasian design.

Pakistani rug, 3'1" x 5'1" New Zealand wool on cotton, 16/18
quality, chrome dyes. Northern Pakistan, Tabriz design.

Pakistani rug, 3'2" x 5'2" New Zealand
wool on cotton, 16/18 quality, chrome
dyes. Northern Pakistan, Tabriz design.

Pakistani rug, 3'1" x 5'2" New Zealand wool on cotton, 16/18 quality, chrome dyes. Northern Pakistan, Tabriz design.

Swat rug, northern Pakistan, 3'3" x 4'5" New Zealand wool on cotton, Vegetal dyes. Caucasian design.

Pakistani rug, 2'2" x 2'9" New Zealand wool on cotton, 11/22 quality, Jaldar design.

Swat rug, northern Pakistan, 2'1" x 3'2" New Zealand wool on cotton, Vegetal dyes. Meshkin design.

Swat rug, northern Pakistan, 2'0" x 3'0" New Zealand wool on cotton, Vegetal dyes. Ahar design.

164

Swat rug, northern Pakistan,
1'10" x 3'0" New Zealand wool
on cotton, Vegetal dyes. Oushak
design.

Swat rug, northern Pakistan, 2'2" x 2'10" New Zealand
wool on cotton, Vegetal dyes. Oushak design.

Swat rug, northern Pakistan,
2'1" x 2'10" New Zealand
wool on cotton, Vegetal dyes.
Ahar design.

Swat rug, northern Pakistan, 1'10"
x 3'1" New Zealand wool on cotton,
Vegetal dyes. Oushak design.

Swat rug, northern Pakistan, 1'10"
x 3'2" New Zealand wool on cotton,
Vegetal dyes. Oushak design.

Swat rug, northern Pakistan,
2'0" x 3'1" New Zealand
wool on cotton, Vegetal dyes.
Oushak design.

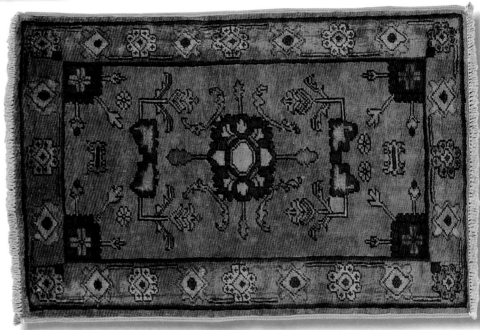

Pakistani rug, 2'1" x 2'9" New Zealand wool on cotton, 11/22 quality, Jaldar design.

Pakistani rug, 3'1" x 4'10" New Zealand wool on cotton, 16/18 quality, chrome dyes, Northern Pakistan, Moghul design.

Pakistani rug, 4'2" x 6'2" New Zealand wool on cotton, 16/18 quality, chrome dyes, Northern Pakistan, Kashan design.

167

Pakistani rug, 3'0" x 5'1" New Zealand wool on cotton, 16/18 quality, chrome dyes, Northern Pakistan, Tabriz design.

Pakistani rug, 3'1" x 5'1" New Zealand wool on cotton, 16/18 quality, chrome dyes, Northern Pakistan, Tabriz design.

Pakistani rug, 6'1" x 9'4" New Zealand wool on cotton, 16/18 quality, chrome dyes,
Northern Pakistan, Tabriz design.

Pakistani rug, 6'1" x 8'8" New
Zealand wool on cotton, 16/18
quality, chrome dyes, Northern
Pakistan, Moghul design.

Pakistani rug, 6'1" x 9'0" New
Zealand wool on cotton, 16/18
quality, chrome dyes, Northern
Pakistan, Tabriz design.

170

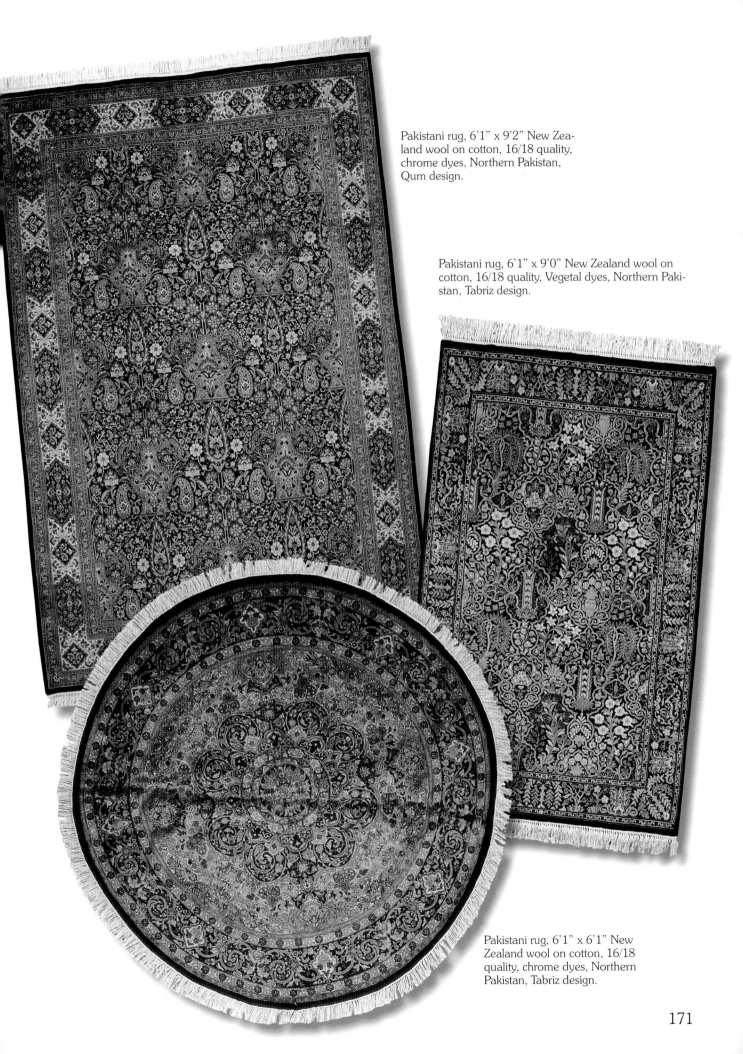

Pakistani rug, 6'1" x 9'2" New Zealand wool on cotton, 16/18 quality, chrome dyes, Northern Pakistan, Qum design.

Pakistani rug, 6'1" x 9'0" New Zealand wool on cotton, 16/18 quality, Vegetal dyes, Northern Pakistan, Tabriz design.

Pakistani rug, 6'1" x 6'1" New Zealand wool on cotton, 16/18 quality, chrome dyes, Northern Pakistan, Tabriz design.

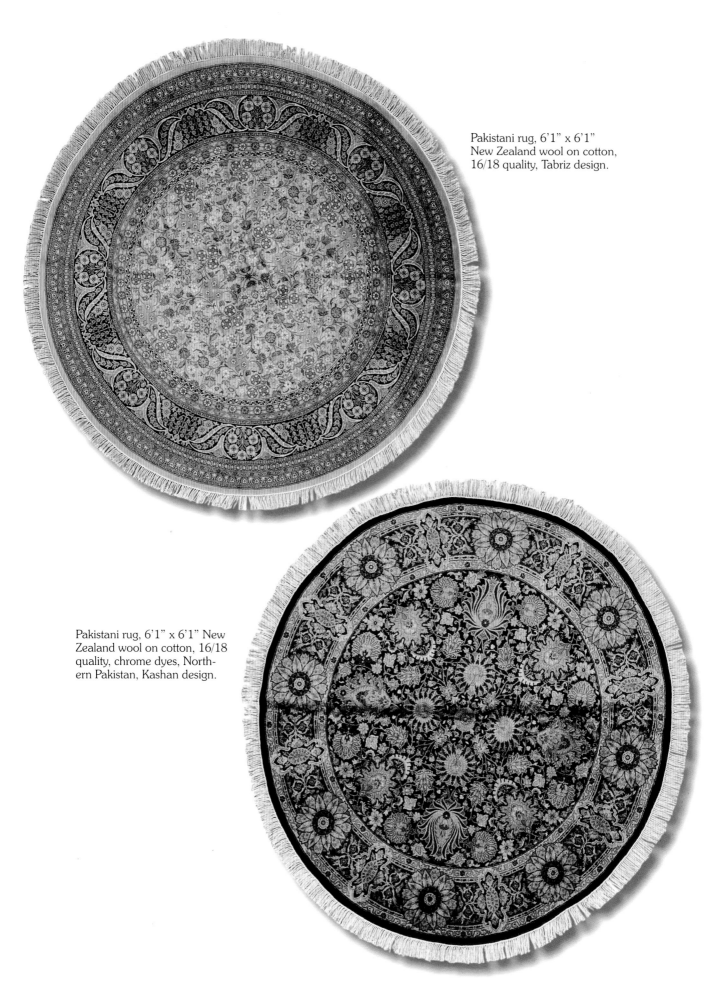

Pakistani rug, 6'1" x 6'1"
New Zealand wool on cotton,
16/18 quality, Tabriz design.

Pakistani rug, 6'1" x 6'1" New
Zealand wool on cotton, 16/18
quality, chrome dyes, Northern Pakistan, Kashan design.

Pakistani rug, 6'8" x 9'8" New
Zealand wool on cotton, 16/18
quality, chrome dyes, Northern
Pakistan, Mahi Tabriz design.

Pakistani rug, 8'1" x 10'1" New
Zealand wool on cotton, 16/18
quality, chrome dyes, Northern
Pakistan, Arles design.

173

Pakistani rug, 4'10" x 6'4"
New Zealand wool on cotton, Vegetal dyes, Gabbeh design.

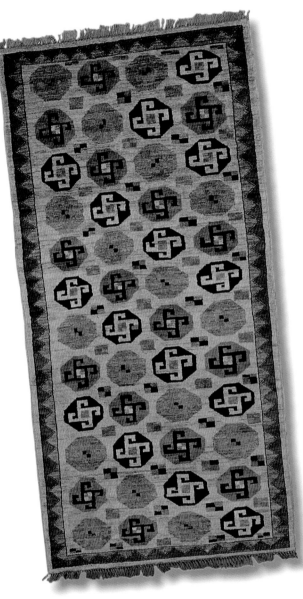

Swat rug, northern Pakistan, 3'1" x 6'4" New Zealand wool on cotton, Vegetal dyes, Caucasian design.

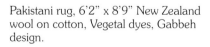

Pakistani rug, 6'2" x 8'9" New Zealand wool on cotton, Vegetal dyes, Gabbeh design.

Swat rug, northern Pakistan,
5'2" x 6'0" New Zealand
wool on cotton, Vegetal dyes,
Caucasian design.

Swat rug, northern
Pakistan, 4'7" x 6'3"
New Zealand wool
on cotton, Vegetal
dyes, Caucasian
design.

Swat rug, northern Pakistan, 4'10"
x 6'6" New Zealand wool on cotton,
Vegetal dyes, Caucasian design.

175

Swat rug, northern Pakistan, 5'4" x 7'2" New Zealand wool and cotton, Vegetal dyes. Shirvan design.

Swat rug, northern Pakistan, 4'5" x 6'6" New Zealand wool and cotton, Vegetal dyes. Avshar design.

Swat rug, northern Pakistan,
4'7" x 7'5" New Zealand
wool on cotton, Vegetal dyes,
Shirvan design.

Pakistani rug, 5'1" x 6'1"
Wool on cotton, Vegetal
dyes, Soumak design.

# Persian Rugs

There has been more written about Persian rugs than any other type of handmade Oriental carpet, due to their rich history and illustrious reputation. Long known for one of the most desirable carpets produced, Iran (also known as Persia in times past) is home to the original Oriental rug. Considered the oldest and most powerful empire in the Middle East, Persia stood at a geographical center, thus a crossroad, of Eastern and Western civilizations. In an area of rich cultural traditions, under the Safavid Dynasty (1502-1736), the region attained its artistic height. All areas of the arts, from calligraphy, architecture, miniature paintings, poetry, and mathematics, flourished here. During this Persian renaissance the Oriental rug gained its widespread reputation when the first carpet workshops were set up in the cities of Kashan, Tabriz, Herat, and Kerman. At this time of great artistic expression, most of the original designs and motifs were established, and they can still be seen today in rugs produced throughout the world.

**Tabriz** is a city in northwestern Iran with a long and popular tradition of rug weaving since the 15th century. A curvilinear design rug it can include center medallions, hunting scenes, prayer rugs and the like. Iranian Tabriz rugs usually have a distinctive double weft which are at times dyed either pale blue or light gray. Today the basic design elements have been mixed with other city patterns in a fusion so that the original designs have been somewhat lost. This is one of the most commonly inspired pattern sources throughout the rug producing regions of the world today

The western market for Persian carpets began in earnest when primarily German and English firms in the mid-19th century set up factory workshops in such cities as Tabriz and Kerman. Soon, enterprising American merchants started importing rugs from the area. From the late 19th century until the 1960s, as their popularity increased, department and furniture stores in the United States imported tens of thousands of Persian rugs.

At the time of this publication, all Persian rugs have increased in value approximately 40%, due to currency conversion to the Euro Standard and inflation.

**Ardabil** is a pattern or design that was originally made in the city of the same name in present day Iran.

**Bakhtiari** is both known as a design and a confederation of tribes covering central and southwestern Iran. One of the best known design elements of these rugs is the compartments filled with colorful garden and animal motifs.

**Bidjar** is both a distinctive design as well as an important center of rug production in northwest Iran, the majority of the population being of Kurdish extraction.

**Farahan** is a region north of the area of Arak in present day Iran. Known from the 19th century onward as a rug producing region, the designs most frequently encountered are Herati and Gol Hinnani. The most commonly seen patterns are of close all over floral motifs such as those seen in Herati patterns.

**Fars** is a large tribal region in Southwestern Iran known for their high quality tribal weavings.

**Gabbeh** is a thick long piled rug woven on horizontal looms by tribes from the Fars region of Iran. Originally intended for their own use they are very popular today in mid century and modern designed environments. The patterns are quite simple and in most cases have small animals such as deer etc. scattered sparingly on a sea of color and are reminiscent of a Mark Rothko painting.

**Genje** is located in Azerbaijan and was famous for the long corridor rugs produced the last quarter of the 19th century using diagonal bars throughout the field.

**Hamadan** located in Iran is an ancient area of rug production and from which the pattern name derives. One of the oldest cities in the world, the designs are composed of geometric patterns.

**Heriz** is one of the most famous and well known rug design produced today with its strong geometric medallion. Once known as a shield pattern, it is still woven today in the villages of Heriz Iran as well as every rug producing area in the world.

**Gorevan** is a type of coarse grade Heriz design rug made in the town by the same name which is located in northwest Iran.

**Isfahan** under Shah Abbas the Great (1588-1629) was the Persian capital. Long known for their rug production some of the earliest designs were borrowed from Chinese porcelain. Today the patterns produced are mainly curvilinear in design and floral in motif.

**Joshagan** is both a pattern and a town in north central Iran. Known for its design of all over lozenge patterns each consisting of a geometric floral motif it is a popular rug and like its big brother the Heriz is found in all major rug producing regions in the world today.

**Mashad** is a city located in Northeastern Iran and is considered a holy city by the Shi'ite people due to the shrine of Imam Reza. A large producer of carpets, the designs most frequently encountered are floral patterns, often coarsely woven.

**Nahavand** is a very historical city located south of Hamedan and is a weaving center known for its distinctive rug sizes of the length being usually twice its width.

**Nain** is south of the Khorassan district in Iran and has a relatively short history of rug production. Beginning right after the Second World War, weavers started producing central medallion rugs in primarily light colors for the western market. The patterns are very similar to Isfahan and are sometimes difficult to differentiate.

**Qum** is a holy city south of Tehran well known for producing very high quality carpets in both wool and silk. Similar to Nain's they are most often seen with striking blue, green, and red colors on an ivory background.

**Sarouk** is one of the most common floral city designs seen in the market today and like its cousin the Tabriz has been fused with other patterns today. A city in Iranian Azerbaijan it has a long history of producing "factory" made rugs for the western market. Today all rug producing regions of the world produce Sarouk patterns.

**Serapi** is a much finer version of its close relation Heriz and was produced from around 1800 to 1930 in the village of Heriz Iran. The original rugs are well known for their rich reddish fields, which are usually framed by blues and whites and are almost always seen with substantial amounts of abrash running throughout the rug. Today the pattern is made in virtually all the rug producing areas of the world.

**Vase Carpets** are a rug that originated in 16th and 17th century Persia with flowers springing from vases. Directional rugs, they are produced in all the major rug producing regions of the world today.

**Yalameh** is an overall term used to describe village rugs from Western Iran which have the design elements of the Lori, Khamseh, and Qashqai people.

**Qashgai** is a large confederacy of tribal people in southwestern Iran. Long known as master weavers especially for their antique tribal rugs, the main design element is a hexagon medallion surrounded by multitudes of small geometric and animal motifs throughout the field. Some of their more recent productions have a colorful barber pole like design as selvage.

• • • • • • • • • • • • • • • • • • • • • • • • • • • • • • • •

**Boteh** is a design element from the Farsi word for immature flower or palm leaf and is a widespread pattern of abstract pine cones, pears, trees, tear drops, or flames.

**Dozar** is a Farsi word used to describe a rug 4" x 6"

**Ghereh** translated means knot in Farsi.

**Mahi** is a Farsi word for a fish design and is composed of a rosette surrounded by leaves, which is usually found inside a diamond shape. A very popular rug design seen today, especially in China.

Rugs have always been an intrinsic part of Iranian culture. During the embargo of goods to the United States beginning with the Iranian Revolution of 1979, rug production waned and Iran lost its preeminence in the rug world. With the lifting of the embargo in 2000, the United States was flooded with low quality Iranian rugs that were made with unsightly electric dyes, bad washing, and boring execution.

While the embargo was in effect, countries such as Pakistan and India improved their rug quality, their understanding of western tastes, and their color palette until Iran became no longer in the forefront. Now, Pakistan produces the most outstanding rugs, with India trailing a close second.

*A word of caution on Iranian rugs*: With the lifting of the embargo, there has been an onslaught of Iranian rugs with harsh and garish colors on the market, the result of using extremely toxic synthetic dyes that result in "electric" colors. We would discourage the consumer from buying these poorly made and inferior goods, due to the dyes and the poor wool quality used in their production; they will not service well.

## The Values of Persian (Iranian) Rugs Today

Because Iran is such a large and diverse area of rug production, it would be impossible to cover prices on all the rugs produced. The following list gives a very rough idea of what you should expect to pay for a rug produced in the last twenty or so years and that is currently available in today's marketplace. Just because a rug has more knots per square inch, it does not always mean it is a better rug. All the knot count indicates is that there is a tighter, crisper pattern and the rug required more weaving hours to produce. If you buy a rug from Iran, try to obtain a carpet with harmonious colors and designs and one free of the electric colors that are found so often today. Because the bulk of rugs contain harsh dyes, always check to see if the rug has not been "chemically washed" to try to remove and tone down the colors. Remember that it is always safest to buy a rug from a reputable dealer in an established firm.

### Pile Rugs
50 to 100 knots per square inch: $10 to $15 per square foot
125 to 150 knots per square inch: $15 to $20 per square foot
150 to 200 knots per square inch: $20 to $25 per square foot
225 to 300 knots per square inch: $30 to $40 per square foot

Fine Silk with 300 knots per square inch: $100 to $200 per square foot
And a 30% premium for rugs made with vegetal dyes.
Add a 20% premium for all rugs with genuine silk touch or outlines.

Persian rug, 4'0" x 6'4" Wool on cotton, Vegetal dyes. Western Iran, Hoseinabad.

Persian rug, 4'8" x 8'6" Wool on cotton, Vegetal dyes. Western Iran, Heriz design.

Persian rug, 3'4" x 5'4" Wool on cotton. Western Iran, Nahavand.

Persian rug, 4'2" x 6'6" Wool on cotton.
Western Iran, Yalameh.

Persian rug, 4'2" x 6'4" Wool on cotton.
Western Iran, Avshar.

Persian rug, 4'4" x 7'0"
Wool on cotton. Western
Iran, Hamadan.

Persian rug, 4'3" x 6'3" Wool on cotton. Western Iran, Senneh.

Persian rug, 5'0" x 8'3" Wool on cotton. Western Iran, Borchalu.

Persian rug, 3'6" x 4'10"
Wool on cotton. Western Iran,
Hamadan.

Persian rug, 4'1" x 6'7" Wool on
cotton. Western Iran, Hoseinabad.

Persian rug, 4'1" x 7'2" Wool on cotton. Western Iran, Hamadan.

Persian rug, 3'8" x 6'1" Wool on cotton. Western Iran, Nahavand.

Persian rug, 4'2" x 7'0" Wool on cotton. Western Iran, Hamadan.

Persian rug, 5'0" x 7'6" Wool
on cotton. Western Iran, Bidjar.

Persian rug, 4'5" x 6'2" Wool
on cotton. Western Iran, Fars.

Persian rug, 4'6" x 6'5"
Wool on cotton. Western
Iran, Nahavard.

Persian rug, 4'0" x 6'4" Wool on cotton.
Western Iran, Hamadan.

Persian rug, 4'2" x 6'9"
Wool on cotton. Western
Iran, Hamadan.

186

Persian rug, 4'7" x 6'9"
Wool on cotton. Western
Iran, Murdsheka.

Persian rug, 4'5" x 7'0" Wool on
cotton. Western Iran, Boteh.

Persian rug, 4'1" x 7'3" Wool on
cotton. Western Iran, Hamadan.

Persian rug, 3'5" x 5'1" Wool on cotton. Western Iran, Hamadan.

Persian rug, 3'7" x 7'5" Wool on cotton. Western Iran, Hamadan.

Persian rug, 3'4" x 4'9" Wool on cotton. Western Iran, Prayer.

Persian rug, 3'9" x 5'10"
Wool on cotton. Western
Iran, Arak.

Persian rug, 4'5" x 7'5"
Wool on cotton. Western
Iran, Hamadan.

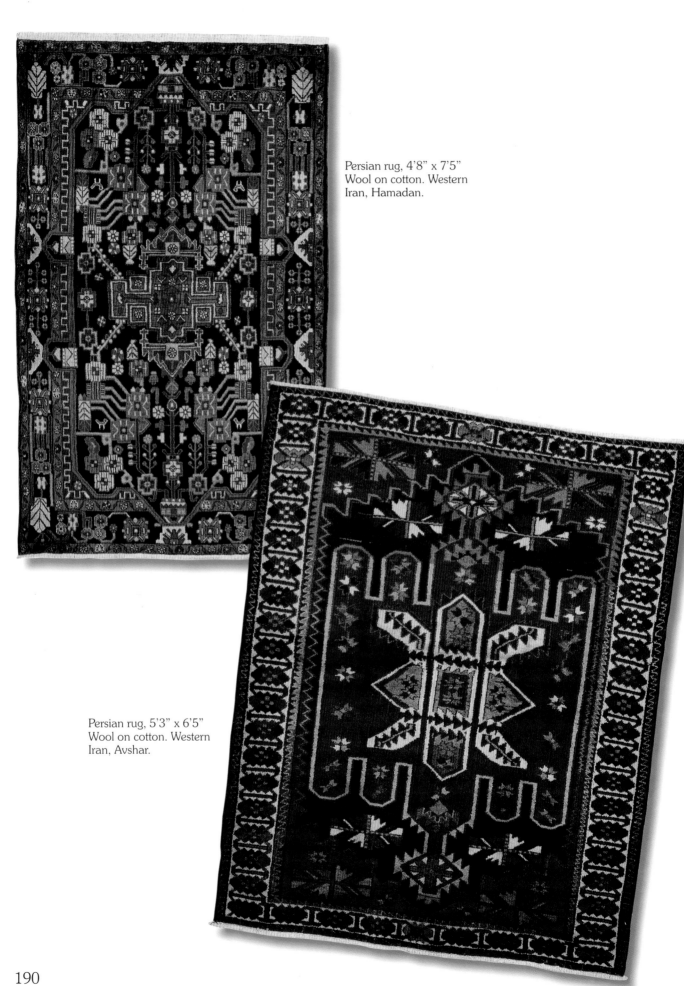

Persian rug, 4'8" x 7'5"
Wool on cotton. Western
Iran, Hamadan.

Persian rug, 5'3" x 6'5"
Wool on cotton. Western
Iran, Avshar.

Persian rug, 5'8" x 6'9"
Wool on cotton. Western
Iran, Hamadan.

Persian rug, 4'6" x 7'9" Wool on
cotton. Western Iran, Hamadan.
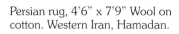

Persian rug, 4'0" x 7'1" Wool on cotton. Western Iran, Hamadan.

Persian rug, 4'10" x 7'5" Wool on cotton. Western Iran, Sarouk.

Persian rug, 2'8" x 3'10" Wool on cotton. Western Iran, Maslaghan.

Persian rug, 5'4" x 7'3" Wool on cotton. Western Iran, Hamadan.

Persian rug, 5'1" x 7'3" Wool on cotton. Western Iran, Sirjan.

Persian rug, 3'4" x 4'8" Wool on wool. Western Iran, Hamadan.

Persian rug, 5'4" x 8'1" Wool on cotton. Western Iran, Afshar.

Persian rug, 3'4" x 4'10"
Wool on cotton. Western
Iran, Hamadan.

Persian rug, 3'3" x 5'4" Wool on cotton.
Western Iran, Hoseinabad.

Persian rug, 3'4" x 4'5" Wool
on cotton. Western Iran,
Hamadan.

Persian rug, 3'6" x 4'9"
Wool on cotton. Western
Iran, Hamadan.

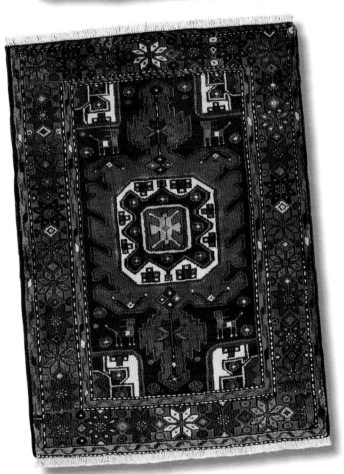

Persian rug, 4'7" x 6'5" Wool on cotton.
Western Iran, Musal.

Persian rug, 3'4" x 4'8"
Wool on cotton. Western
Iran, Hamadan.

Persian rug, 2'8" x 4'1" Wool on cotton. Western Iran, Hamadan.

Persian rug, 3'3" x 5'1" Wool on cotton. Western Iran, Hamadan.

Persian rug, 2'8" x 4'1" Wool on cotton. Western Iran, Hamadan.

Persian rug, 3'1" x 4'2"
Wool on cotton. Western
Iran, Hamadan.

Persian rug, 2'7" x 4'2" Wool on cotton. Western Iran,
Hamadan.

Persian rug, 2'7" x 4'1"
Wool on cotton. Western
Iran, Hamadan.

Persian rug, 3'7" x 4'5" Wool on cotton. Western Iran, Hamadan.

Persian rug, 3'3" x 5'1" Wool on cotton. Western Iran, Hamadan.

Persian rug, 3'9" x 5'3" Wool on cotton. Western Iran, Sarouk.

Persian rug, 3'3" x 5'3" Wool on cotton. Western Iran, Musal.

Persian rug, 3'5" x 5'5" Wool on cotton. Western Iran, Hamadan.

Persian rug, 5'2" x 7'4"
Wool on cotton. Western
Iran, Hamadan.

Persian rug, 3'6" x 5'1"
Wool on cotton. Western
Iran, Lars.

Persian rug, 3'4" x 5'2"
Wool on cotton. Western
Iran, Hamadan.

Persian rug, 3'6" x 4'10" Wool on cotton.
Western Iran, Hamadan.

Persian rug, 3'9" x 5'2"
Wool on cotton. Western
Iran, Hamadan.

Persian rug, 3'8" x 5'4" Wool on cotton. Western Iran, Hamadan.

Persian rug, 4'2" x 8'3" Wool on cotton. Western Iran, Kellegh.

Persian rug, 4'9" x 8'2"
Wool on cotton. Western
Iran, Hamadan.

Persian rug, 4'3" x 8'5"
Wool on cotton. Western
Iran, Kellegh.

205

Persian rug, 4'4" x 7'5" Wool on cotton. Western Iran, Hamadan.

Persian rug, 4'8" x 5'9" Wool on cotton. Western Iran, Ardebil.

Persian rug, 5'1" x 7'4" Wool on cotton. Central Iran, Meimei.

Persian rug, 5'6" x 9'6" Wool on cotton, Vegetal dyes. Western Iran, Sarouk.

Persian rug, 4'8" x 8'6" Wool on cotton. Western Iran, Kellegh.

Persian rug, 8'2" x 16'5" Wool on cotton, Vegetal dyes. Northwestern Iran, Heriz.

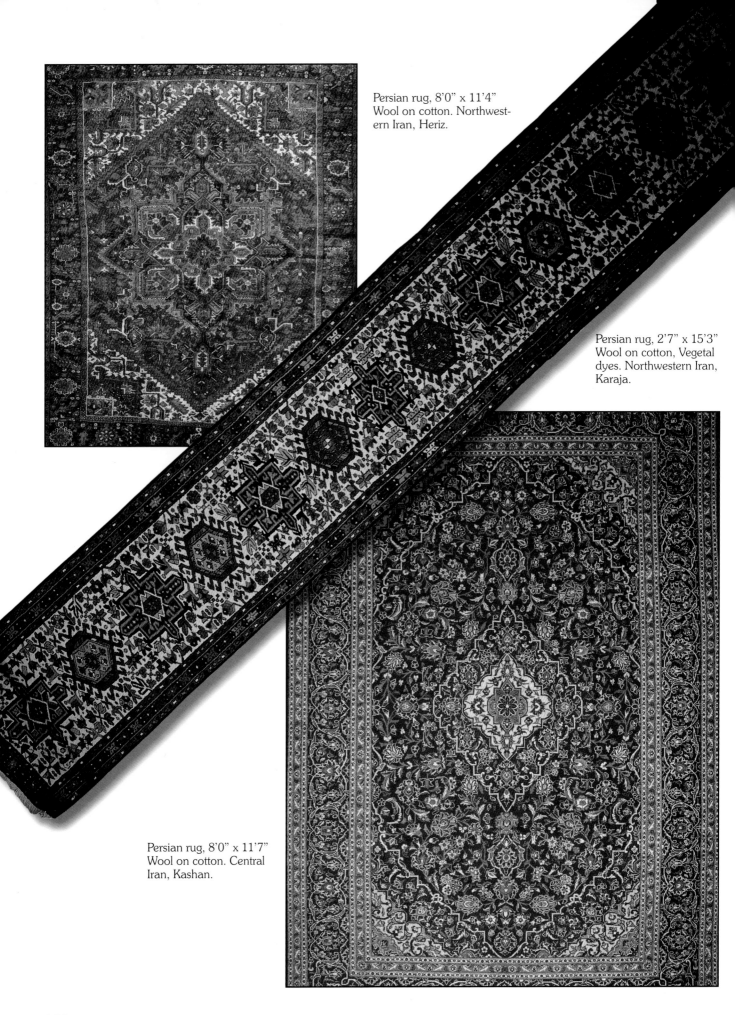

Persian rug, 8'0" x 11'4"
Wool on cotton. Northwestern Iran, Heriz.

Persian rug, 2'7" x 15'3"
Wool on cotton, Vegetal dyes. Northwestern Iran, Karaja.

Persian rug, 8'0" x 11'7"
Wool on cotton. Central Iran, Kashan.

Persian rug, 8'3" x 11'4"
Wool on cotton. Central Iran,
Joshgahan.

Persian rug,
9'10" x 10'4"
Wool on cotton.
Northwestern
Iran, Tabriz.

Persian rug, 4'0" x 6'0" Wool on cotton.
Western Iran, Gabbeh.

Persian rug, 6'5" x 9'10"
Wool on cotton. Western
Iran, Tabriz.

Persian rug, 4'9" x 4'9" Silk
on silk. Central Iran, Qum.

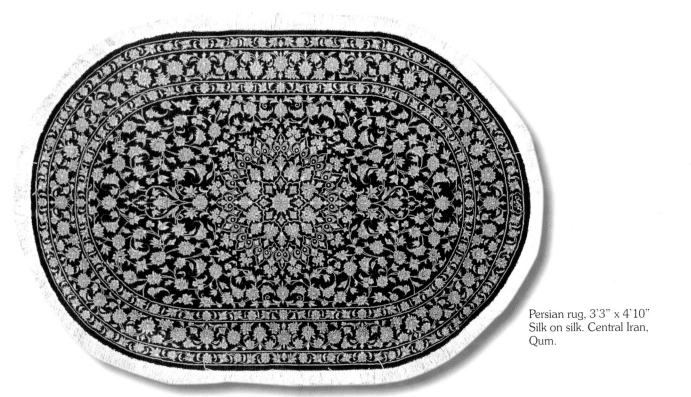

Persian rug, 3'3" x 4'10"
Silk on silk. Central Iran,
Qum.

Persian rug, 3'4" x 4'8" Wool and silk pile on cotton. Central Iran,
Nain.

Persian rug, 3'4" x 4'10" Wool and silk pile on cotton. Central Iran,
Nain.

Persian rug, 4'2" x 6'8" Silk on silk. Central Iran, Tabriz Hunt Scene.

Persian rug, 2'8" x 4'3" Wool on cotton. Northwestern Iran, Tabriz.

Persian rug, 1'10" x 2'7" Silk on silk. Central Iran, Qum.

Persian rug, 2'1" x 3'1" Wool on cotton. Western Iran, Bakhtiari.

# Tibetan Rugs

This is one of the most misleading areas of rug production today. Tibetan rugs should, in fact, be labeled Nepalese rugs. Due to the political turmoil in Tibet from 1959 through the early 1960s, thousands of Tibetan people fled to nearby Nepal and settled in the Katmandu valley. For centuries, there was a long tradition in Tibet of making rugs as saddle blankets, bedding, and meditation mats in monasteries. This tradition was carried to Nepal. The newly arrived refugees took up a whole-hearted cottage industry in rug making, as a means of making a living and with Swiss support. Originally designed as a business model to supply the growing tourist industry in Nepal, rug making soon blossomed as German buyers came into the area in the 1970s asking for larger non-traditional sizes. As a result, the famous plain field rugs started appearing. Beginning in the 1990s and with widespread promotion, several United States importers encouraged weavers to fill the growing demand from the high end designer market. Today, the rug industry is in full swing in Nepal, with large amounts of plain and modern designs being exported to the burgeoning western market.

## Values of Tibetan Rugs Today

### Pile Rugs
60 knots per square inch: $20 to $25 per square foot
100 knots per square inch: $35 to $45 per square foot

Add 20% premium for rugs made with vegetal dyes

Tibetan rug, 3'0" x 6'0" Wool on wool, Dragon design.

Tibetan rug, 2'0" x 3'1" Wool on wool, Tiger design.

Tibetan rug, 6'8" x 9'4"
Wool on cotton, hand knotted in Nepal.

Tibetan rug, 4'3" x 7'1"
Wool on cotton, hand
knotted in Nepal.

Tibetan rug, 5'1" x 7'9"
Wool on cotton, hand
knotted in Nepal.

Tibetan rug, 6'2" x 9'4"
Wool on cotton, hand
knotted in Nepal.

Tibetan rug, 4'2" x 6'6"
Wool on cotton, hand
knotted in Nepal.

Tibetan rug, 6'4" x 9'6"
Wool on cotton, hand
knotted in Nepal.

216

Left: Tibetan rug, 2'10" x 9'6" Wool on cotton, hand made in Nepal.
Right: Tibetan rug, 2'6" x 10'2" Wool on cotton, hand knotted in Nepal.

Tibetan rug, 5'10" x 8'7" Wool on cotton, hand knotted in Nepal.

Tibetan rug, 4'1" x 9'4" Wool on cotton, hand knotted in Nepal.

Tibetan rug, 3'3" x 5'2"
Wool on cotton, hand knotted in Nepal.

Tibetan rug, 4'2" x 5'9" Wool on cotton,
hand knotted in Nepal.

Tibetan rug, 3'10" x 5'4"
Wool on cotton, hand
knotted in Nepal.

# Turkish Rugs

The first western documentation of rug production in present day Turkey occurred when the Italian traveler, Marco Polo, described the wide variety of carpets he encountered after his visit to Anatolia in 1271. He claimed that Turkish geometric and animal patterns were the most beautiful in the world. But, as in nearby Persia, the art of carpet weaving had been well established in Turkey for hundreds of years prior to his visit.

**Ghiordes** is a town in western Turkey most famous for their production of small prayer rugs.

**Hereke** located in western Turkey, it is considered the finest weaving center in the entire country. Well known for their fine wool and pure silk rugs the area has been synonymous with quality since the days of the Ottoman Empire.

**Konya** is a famous Turkish town well known for their prayer rugs and small mats. Flat woven kilims are also a distinct product from the area as well.

**Ladik** is a Turkish center for carpets beginning in the 18th century. Known for its distinctive designs of arched mihrabs, today it still produces kilims and pile carpets.

**Melas** is a town located in southwestern Turkey well known for their finely woven designs incorporating the Mihrab.

**Ushak** is a famous town in west central Turkey long known for their distinctive designs in carpets. Since the end of the 19th century the area has produced large room size rugs for the Western market and are made with wool pile on a wool foundation. Most of the designs encountered are standard medallions or all over patterns and are popular with today's decorators. Some of the most spectacular of the modern Ushaks being produced are coming out of Pakistan using high quality wool and vegetal dyes to recreate their antique Turkish counterparts.

Some of the more popular and famous pile rugs produced in Turkey include fine Herekes, in both wool and silk, also Ladik, Kars, Kula, Konya, Kayseri, Milas Yagcibedir, Yahyali designs, just to name a few. Also, in the last two decades there has been a resurgence of superb vegetal dyed rugs, beginning with the Dobag project. Several firms, such as Black Mountain and Asia Minor have been producing beautiful re-creations of such ancient patterns as Avshars and other designs from the Ottoman empire.

**Avshar** a type of carpet made by Turkish speaking nomads who primarily occupied the area around present day city of Kerman, Iran. Named after the famous leader of the tribe Nader Shah (1736-1747) they are well known for their subtle geometric patterns.

**Caucasian** is a loose term for rugs and designs produced in the area of the Caucasus Mountains in Southern Russia.

**Herati** is said to be an old Turkish pattern that had originally been composed of abstract designs of fish and turtles. Today it is most often seen in a repeated field design of a flower centered in a diamond with curled leaves located outside the diamond and parallel to the sides.

**Kazak** designates a very popular bold geometric pattern that today is mainly woven in Turkey and Peshawar Pakistan. Long favored by real rug connoisseurs, the original Kazaks were produced by Azeri Turks, Armenians, Albanians and Northern Caucasian people with the center of production based in the city of the same name located in Northwest Azerbaijan. Examples from the 19th century and before are eagerly competed for by collectors everywhere at the major auction houses of the world.

**Yastik** is a type of Turkish rug usually used as a pillow cover and has a very distinctive size of approximately 1 by 3 feet.

Flat woven rugs, or kilims, also have a long history in the Turkish countryside and are produced in a wide assortment of colors and designs. Some of the more commonly seen patterns include Aksaray, Aydin, Besarabian, Kars, Konya, and Sivas, just to name a few.

**Flatweave** is a knotless way of weaving where the warp strands are used as the foundation and the weft strands are used in creating patterns and the foundation of the rug. Most commonly seen flat weaves are dhurries and kilims.

**Kilim** is a flat woven rug constructed using weft yarns which face the flat looped area of the rug.

**Besarabian** is a type of kilim originally woven in Romania but now found in Turkey as well. Designs that are usually encountered are strong floral motifs with the rose being the most prevalent with the color black used as background highlight.

Today, the beautiful country of Turkey produces a wide variety of rugs and actually is the largest retail rug marketplace in the world. Because of this, few dealers import Turkish rugs into the United States; the suppliers would rather sell their goods to foreign visitors at inflated prices. This reason and the local currency fluctuations make Turkish goods far too expensive to import. Countless tourists flock to well-known areas, such as the Grand Bazaar of Istanbul, in search of rugs at what they believe to be truly low prices. Yet, in reality, they end up paying far more than they would pay from a well-established and reputable retailer in the United States or Europe for rugs of comparable quality. On a recent trip to Turkey, we found a tremendous amount of low quality Iranian rugs flooding the marketplace as well as Chinese silk rugs being sold as Hereke silk and mercerized cotton rugs being sold as silk. When you buy rugs overseas, you have absolutely no recourse; it is always best not to be tempted, but just to look and enjoy the sights and sounds of this beautiful country.

---

**Hali** is a Turkish word for carpet or rug.

**Yuruk** is a Turkish word for nomad.

---

**William Morris** (1834-1896) was a British craftsman, designer, writer, topographer, and socialist whose firm adopted Middle Eastern designs to western tastes. Today the term has been applied to designs in a variety of rugs and is associated with the arts and crafts design movement.

## The Values of Turkish Rugs Today

The following values are for Turkish rugs most frequently encountered in today's marketplace.

### Pile Rugs
Wool Hereke: $35 to $45 per square foot
Silk Hereke $200 to $300 per square foot
Kayseri, Kula, Ladik: $20 to $30 per square foot
Konya, Kula, Milas, Yagcibedir, Yahyali: $15 to $25 per square foot

*Add a 20% premium to above rugs made with vegetal dyes*

Ottoman, Avshar, etc. vegetal dye: $45 to $55 per square foot

### Flatwoven Rugs
Kilims are made in a wide range of patterns and designs.
New coarse weave rugs made with poor quality, underfat wool: $5 to $8 per square foot
Finer weave kilims: $15 to $25 per square foot
Floral Besarabian: $20 to $30 per square foot

*Add a premium of 20% for all Kilims made with vegetal dyes.*

Turkish rug, 8'2" x 10'3"
Wool on cotton, Vegetal dyes.
Oushak design.

Turkish rug, 9'1" x 11'10"
Wool on cotton, Vegetal dyes.
Oushak design.

Turkish rug, 7'9" x 10'2"
Wool on cotton, Vegetal dyes
Oushak design.

Turkish rug, 5'10" x 9'7" Wool on cotton, Vegetal dyes. Besarabian design.

Turkish rug, 8'1" x 10'3" Wool on cotton, Vegetal dyes. Ottoman design.

Turkish rug, 7'3" x 11'7"
Wool on cotton, Vegetal
dyes. Anatolian Kilim.

Turkish rug, 8'6" x 10'2"
Wool on cotton, Vegetal dyes.
Sultanabad design.

Turkish rug, 8'1" x 9'10"
Wool on cotton, Vegetal
dyes. Oushak design.

Turkish rug, 7'9" x 9'8" Wool
on cotton, Vegetal dyes.
Oushak design.

# chapter
## 25

Over the next few days, Mom and Dad called no less than twelve times. Each time they both got on the phone, doubling up, as if it might increase their persuasive powers. Each time I assured them over and over again that yes, I knew what I was doing, and that yes, I was still staying. Surprisingly, it wasn't as difficult as I thought it would be. My throat ached when Mom cried and I closed my eyes when Dad swore, but I held fast. It was as if a wedge had already been driven between us; something built out of necessity, but there nonetheless. I wasn't going to be the one to knock it back down. Not after all this time.

And to make sure of that, on the third day I turned my phone off completely and shoved it under my pillow.

———

Sophie and I worked on the outside of the house for the rest of the week. While I scraped, I thought about Maggie. Especially that black mohawk hair of hers. I wondered who in the family she resembled the most. Mom? Dad? Sophie? Me, possibly?